Information Security Handbook

Develop a threat model and incident response strategy
to build a strong information security framework

Darren Death

BIRMINGHAM - MUMBAI

Information Security Handbook

First published: December 2017

Production reference: 1071217

Published by Packt Publishing Ltd.
Livery Place
35 Livery Street
Birmingham
B3 2PB, UK.

ISBN 978-1-78847-883-0

www.packtpub.com

Credits

Author
Darren Death

Reviewers
Abhinav Rai
Heath Renfrow

Commissioning Editor
Gebin George

Acquisition Editor
Herambh Bhavsar

Content Development Editor
Abhishek Jadhav

Technical Editor
Mohd Riyan Khan

Copy Editor
Safis Editing

Project Coordinator
Judie Jose

Proofreader
Safis Editing

Indexer
Pratik Shirodkar

Graphics
Tania Dutta

Production Coordinator
Aparna Bhagat

About the Author

Darren Death is an information security professional living in the DC Metropolitan Area. During his 17-year technology career, he has supported the private and public sector at the local, state, and national levels. Darren has worked for organizations such as the Department of Justice, Library of Congress, and the Federal Emergency Management Agency. Darren currently works for Artic Slope Regional Corporation as its chief information security officer. In this role, Darren is responsible for the ASRC Enterprise Information Security program, where he manages the Information Security program across the 3 billion dollar ASRC portfolio crossing many business sectors to include energy, financial services, hospitality, retail, construction, and federal government contracting.

Darren is very active in the information security community and can be heard at many conferences throughout the year speaking on many of the topics covered in this book. Infragard is an organization that is dedicated to sharing information and intelligence working to prevent hostile acts against the United States. In this role, he teaches students the building blocks that go into establishing a successful information security program.

I would like to thank my amazing wife and children for putting up with me and sacrificing the time that it took to write this book.

I would also like to thank the many executives that have walked alongside me throughout my career. These executives include: Leif Henecke, CIO at ASRC Federal; Ann-Marie Massenberg, Chief of Staff at the Office of Financial Management at the US Department of Transportation; Jonathan Alboum, CIO at USDA; Steve Elky, Director of IT Strategic Planning at the Library of Congress; Douglas Ament, CIO at the US Copyright Office; Kyle Holtzman, Deputy Assistant Director of Service Portfolio Management at the U.S. Department of Justice; and Oscar Jordan, Master Sergeant United States Air Force.

Without learning the valuable lessons that I learned from these professionals, I would not be where I am today. It is also because of these individuals that I strongly support and participate in mentoring opportunities for others who are staring in their IT careers and work to teach and spread what I have learned to others regarding IT and Information Security best practices.

About the Reviewers

Abhinav Rai has been associated with information security professional and has experience in web application security, network security, mobile application security, web services security, source code review, and configuration audit. He is currently working as an information security professional.

He has completed his degree in computer science and his postgraduate diploma in IT infrastructure, systems and security. He also holds a certificate in communication protocol design and testing. He can be reached at `abhinav.rai.55@gmail.com`.

Mr. Heath Renfrow has served the Chief Information Security Officer for multiple global organizations, and most recently as the CISO for United States Army Medicine, where he was awarded the 2017 Global CISO of the year by EC-COUNCIL, the largest cyber training body in the world. Mr. Renfrow has 20 years of global cyber security professional experience, and is considered one of the leading cyber experts today. He holds Bachelors in Science in Information Technology, and a Master's of Science in Cyber Studies. Mr. Renfrow also holds numerous industry leading certifications, including Certified Chief Information Security Officer (C|CISO), Certified Information Systems Security Professional (CISSP), and Certified Ethical Hacker (C|EH).

All praise to my Lord and Savior, and as always a thank you to my loving and supportive wife, Kathy, as I would be nothing without both!

www.PacktPub.com

For support files and downloads related to your book, please visit www.PacktPub.com.

Did you know that Packt offers eBook versions of every book published, with PDF and ePub files available? You can upgrade to the eBook version at www.PacktPub.com and as a print book customer, you are entitled to a discount on the eBook copy. Get in touch with us at service@packtpub.com for more details.

At www.PacktPub.com, you can also read a collection of free technical articles, sign up for a range of free newsletters and receive exclusive discounts and offers on Packt books and eBooks.

https://www.packtpub.com/mapt

Get the most in-demand software skills with Mapt. Mapt gives you full access to all Packt books and video courses, as well as industry-leading tools to help you plan your personal development and advance your career.

Why subscribe?

- Fully searchable across every book published by Packt
- Copy and paste, print, and bookmark content
- On demand and accessible via a web browser

Customer Feedback

Thanks for purchasing this Packt book. At Packt, quality is at the heart of our editorial process. To help us improve, please leave us an honest review of this book's Amazon page at https://www.amazon.com/dp/1788478835/.

If you'd like to join our team of regular reviewers, you can e-mail us at customerreviews@packtpub.com. We award our regular reviewers with free eBooks and videos in exchange for their valuable feedback. Help us be relentless in improving our products!

Table of Contents

Preface

Information security has become a global challenge that is impacting organizations across every industry sector. C-Suite and board level executives are beginning to take their obligations seriously and as a result require competent business-focused advice and guidance from the organization's information security professionals. Being able to establish a fully developed, risk-based, and business-focused information security program to support your organization is critical to ensuring your organization's success moving into the future.

In this book, we will explore what it takes to establish an information security program that covers the following aspects:

- Focusing on business alignment, engagement, and support
- Utilizing risk-based methodologies
- Establishing effective organizational communication
- Implementing foundational information security hygiene practices
- Implementing information security program best practices

What this book covers

Chapter 1, *Information and Data Security Fundamentals*, provides the reader with an overview of key concepts that will be examined throughout this book. The reader will understand the history, key concepts, components of information, and data security. Additionally, the reader will understand how these concepts should balance with business needs.

Chapter 2, *Defining the Threat Landscape*, understanding the modern threat landscape, helps you as the information security professional in developing a highly effective information security program that can mount a secure defense against modern adversaries in support of your organization's business/mission goals and objectives. In this chapter, you will learn: How to determine what is important to your organization, potential threats to your organization, Types of hackers/adversaries, methods used by the hacker/adversary, and methods of conducting training and awareness as it relates to threats.

Chapter 3, *Preparing for Information and Data Security*, helps you to learn the important activities required to establish an enterprise-wide information security program with a focus on executive buy-in, policies, procedures, standards, and guidelines. Additionally, you will learn: Planning concepts associated with information security program establishment; Information security program success factors; SDLC Integration of the information security program; Information security program maturity concepts; and best practices related to policies, procedures, standards, and guidelines.

Chapter 4, *Information Security Risk Management*, explains the fundamentals of information security risk management, which provides the main interface for prioritization and communication between the information security program and the business. Additionally, you will learn: Key information security risk management concepts; How to determine where valuable data is in your organization; Quick risk assessment techniques; How risk management affects different parts of the organization; How to perform information categorization; Security control selection, implementation, and testing; and Authorizing information systems for production operations.

Chapter 5, *Developing Your Information and Data Security Plan*, speaks about the concepts necessary to develop your information security program plan. Your program plan will be a foundational document that will establish how your information security program will function and interact with the rest of the business. Additionally, you will learn: How to develop the objectives for your information security program, elements of a successful information security program, information security program business / mission alignment, information security program plan elements, and establishing information security program enforcement.

Chapter 6, *Continuous Testing and Monitoring*, explains that it is important for the information security professional to understand that vulnerabilities in information system are a fact of life that is not going away anytime soon. The key to protecting the modern information system is continued vigilance through continuous technical testing. In this chapter, you will learn: Technical testing capabilities at your disposal, Testing integration into the SDLC, Continuous monitoring considerations, Vulnerability assessment considerations, and Penetration testing considerations.

Chapter 7, *Business Continuity/Disaster Recovery Planning*, encompasses two separate but related disciplines that work together. Business Continuity Planning serves to ensure that an organization can effectively understand what business processes and information are important to the continued operations and success of the organization. Disaster Recovery Planning serves to develop a technical solution that supports the business needs of the organization in the event of a system outage. In this chapter, you will learn: The scope and focus areas of the BCDR plan and designing, implementing, testing, and maintaining the BCDR plan.

Chapter 8, *Incident Response Planning*, speaks about an incident response plan and procedures that your information security program implements to ensure that you have adequate and repeatable processes in place to respond to an information security incident that occurs against your organizational network or information systems. In this chapter, you will learn: Why you need an incident response plan, What components make up the incident response plan, Tools and techniques related to incident response, The incident response process, and the OODA loop and how it can be applied to incident response.

Chapter 9, *Developing a Security Operations Center*, serves as your centralized view into your enterprise information systems. The security operations center goal is to ensure that this view is real-time so that your organization can identify and respond to internal and external threats as quickly as possible. In this chapter, you will learn: What comprises the responsibilities of the security operations center; security operations center tool management and design; security operations center roles, processes, and procedures; and internal versus outsourced security operations center implementation considerations.

Chapter 10, *Developing an Information Security Architecture Program*, explains that Security Architecture establishes rigorous and comprehensive policies, procedures, and guidelines around the development and operationalization of an Information Security Architecture across the enterprise information technology deployed within an organization. Additionally, you will learn about: Incorporating security architecture into the system development life cycle process, conducting an initial information security analysis, and Developing a security architecture advisement program.

Chapter 11, *Cloud Security Consideration*, enables on-demand and ubiquitous access to a shared pool of configurable outsourced computing resources such as networks, servers, storage, and applications. In this chapter, you will learn: cloud computing characteristics; Cloud computing service, deployment, and management models; and Special information security consideration as it relates to Cloud Computing.

Chapter 12, *Information and Data Security Best Practices,* speaks about a selection of best practices to help ensure the overall information security health of your organization's information systems. The topics covered in this chapter include information security best practices related to: user account security, least functionality, updates and patching, secure configurations, application security, and network security.

What you need for this book

This book will guide you through the installation of all the tools that you need to follow the examples. You will need to install Webstorm version 10 to effectively run the code samples present in this book.

Who this book is for

This book is targeted at the information security professional looking to understand the key success factors needed to build a successful business-aligned information security program. Additionally, this book is well suited for anyone looking to understand the key aspects of an information security program and how they should be implemented within an organizational culture.

Conventions

In this book, you will find a number of text styles that distinguish between different kinds of information. Here are some examples of these styles and an explanation of their meaning. Code words in text, database table names, folder names, filenames, file extensions, pathnames, dummy URLs, user input, and Twitter handles are shown as follows: "The next lines of code read the link and assign it to the `<script>123</script>`.

New terms and **important words** are shown in bold.

Warnings or important notes appear like this.

Tips and tricks appear like this.

Reader feedback

Feedback from our readers is always welcome. Let us know what you think about this book-what you liked or disliked. Reader feedback is important for us as it helps us develop titles that you will really get the most out of. To send us general feedback, simply email feedback@packtpub.com, and mention the book's title in the subject of your message. If there is a topic that you have expertise in and you are interested in either writing or contributing to a book, see our author guide at www.packtpub.com/authors.

Customer support

Now that you are the proud owner of a Packt book, we have a number of things to help you to get the most from your purchase.

Downloading the color images of this book

We also provide you with a PDF file that has color images of the screenshots/diagrams used in this book. The color images will help you better understand the changes in the output. You can download this file from https://www.packtpub.com/sites/default/files/downloads/InformationSecurityHandbook_ColorImages.pdf.

Errata

Although we have taken every care to ensure the accuracy of our content, mistakes do happen. If you find a mistake in one of our books-maybe a mistake in the text or the code-we would be grateful if you could report this to us. By doing so, you can save other readers from frustration and help us improve subsequent versions of this book. If you find any errata, please report them by visiting http://www.packtpub.com/submit-errata, selecting your book, clicking on the **Errata Submission Form** link, and entering the details of your errata. Once your errata are verified, your submission will be accepted and the errata will be uploaded to our website or added to any list of existing errata under the Errata section of that title. To view the previously submitted errata, go to https://www.packtpub.com/books/content/support and enter the name of the book in the search field. The required information will appear under the **Errata** section.

Piracy

Piracy of copyrighted material on the internet is an ongoing problem across all media. At Packt, we take the protection of our copyright and licenses very seriously. If you come across any illegal copies of our works in any form on the internet, please provide us with the location address or website name immediately so that we can pursue a remedy. Please contact us at copyright@packtpub.com with a link to the suspected pirated material. We appreciate your help in protecting our authors and our ability to bring you valuable content.

Questions

If you have a problem with any aspect of this book, you can contact us at questions@packtpub.com, and we will do our best to address the problem.

1

Information and Data Security Fundamentals

Computers have been instrumental to human progress for more than half a century. As these devices have become more sophisticated they have come under increasing attack from those looking to disrupt organizations using these systems. From the first boot sector virus to advanced, highly-complex, nation-state threats, the ability for an adversary to negatively impact an organization has never been greater. While the attacker has become more sophisticated, our ability to prepare for and defend against the attacker has also become very sophisticated. Throughout this book, I will discuss what it takes to establish an information security program that helps to ensure an organization is properly defended.

The first chapter will provide the reader with an overview of key concepts that will be examined throughout this book. The reader will learn the history, key concepts, components of information, and data security. Additionally, the reader will understand how these concepts should balance with business needs.

The topics covered in this chapter include the following:

- Information security challenges
- The evolution of cybercrime
- The modern role of information security:
    - IT security engineering
    - Information assurance
    - The CIA triad
- Organizational information security assessments
- Risk management

- Information security standards
- Policies
- Training

Information security challenges

The threats faced by today's organizations are highly complex and represent a real danger. The ability to mount an attack has become very simple due to many factors including the following:

- **End user**: End users that use our information systems are prone to clicking on website URLs and launching attachments in emails
- **Malware kits**: Paying hackers for DIY kits to easily develop your own malware
- **Cloud computing**: Cheap and easy access to computing resources helps to ensure easy access to processing power
- **Exploit subscription services**: Underground services that an attacker can subscribe to, to get the latest exploits

An attacker can take these tools, string them together with tutorials found online (as well as their own knowledge and resources), and build a sophisticated attack that could affect millions of computers worldwide.

Modern computer systems were never really developed to be secure. From the very beginning, computers have had an inherent trust factor built into them. Designers did not take into account the fact that adversaries might exploit their systems to harvest the valuable assets they contained. Security therefore, came in the form of bolt-ons or bandages, for solving an inherent problem. This still continues to this day. If you look at a modern computer science program, cybersecurity is often not included. This leads us to the modern internet, overflowing with vulnerable software and operating systems that require constant patches because security has always been an afterthought. Instead of security being built into an information system from the beginning, we are faced with an epidemic of vulnerable systems around the world.

The computer power of the average individual has greatly increased over the past few decades. This has resulted in an increase of sanctioned, and unsanctioned, personally-owned devices processing organizational data and being connected to corporate networks. All of these unmanaged devices are often set up to accommodate speed and convenience for a personal user and do not take into account the requirements of corporate information security.

Many organizations see information security as a hindrance to productivity. It is common to see business leaders, as well as IT personnel, avoid the discussion surrounding security with the fear that security will prevent the corporation from achieving its mission. Implementing security within a project **Systems Development Life Cycle** (**SDLC**) may be fought against, as team members may believe security will prevent a project from being completed on time or viewed as an impediment to a business' financial gain. Tools such as **multi-factor authentication** (**MFA**) or **Virtual Private Networks** (**VPN**) may be resisted as the business might not want to invest the capital for such solutions, due to not understanding the technology and how it would minimize the cyber risk posture of the organization.

Overcoming these challenges requires that the information security leader has a strong understanding of the organizations that they work for and that communication is effectively maintained. The information security professional must integrate with all functional/business owners within their organization. This will allow the security professional to help determine the risk posture of each business area, and help the business owner make sound risk-based decisions. Information security must offer solutions to the business leader's challenges versus adding new challenges for the business leader to solve. Additionally, the information security professional must work and collaborate effectively with their counterparts in information technology. Many information security professionals focus on dictating policy without discussing what is actually needed. Work to foster a relationship where the information security group is sought out for answers rather than avoided.

Evolution of cybercrime

As computer systems have now become integral to the daily functioning of businesses, organizations, governments, and individuals we have learned to put a tremendous amount of trust in these systems. As a result, we have placed incredibly important and valuable information on them. History has shown, that things of value will always be a target for a criminal. Cybercrime is no different. As people flood their personal computers, phones, and so on with valuable data, they put a target on that information for the criminal to aim for, in order to gain some form of profit from the activity. In the past, in order for a criminal to gain access to an individual's valuables, they would have to conduct a robbery in some shape or form. In the case of data theft, the criminal would need to break into a building, sifting through files looking for the information of greatest value and profit. In our modern world, the criminal can attack their victims from a distance, and due to the nature of the internet, these acts would most likely never meet retribution.

In the 70s, we saw criminals taking advantage of the tone system used on phone networks. The attack was called *phreaking*, where the attacker reverse-engineered the tones used by the telephone companies to make long distance calls.

In 1988, the first computer worm made its debut on the internet and caused a great deal of destruction to organizations. This first worm was called the **Morris worm**, after its creator Robert Morris. While this worm was not originally intended to be malicious it still caused a great deal of damage. The *U.S. Government Accountability Office* in 1980 estimated that the damage could have been as high as $10,000,000.00.

1989 brought us the first known ransomware attack, which targeted the healthcare industry. Ransomware is a type of malicious software that locks a user's data, until a small ransom is paid, which will result in the issuance of a cryptographic unlock key. In this attack, an evolutionary biologist named Joseph Popp distributed 20,000 floppy disks across 90 countries, and claimed the disk contained software that could be used to analyze an individual's risk factors for contracting the AIDS virus. The disk however contained a malware program that when executed, displayed a message requiring the user to pay for a software license. Ransomware attacks have evolved greatly over the years with the healthcare field still being a very large target.

The 90s brought the web browser and email to the masses, which meant new tools for cybercriminals to exploit. This allowed the cybercriminal to greatly expand their reach. Up till this time, the cybercriminal needed to initiate a physical transaction, such as providing a floppy disk. Now cybercriminals could transmit virus code over the internet in these new, highly vulnerable web browsers. Cybercriminals took what they had learned previously and modified it to operate over the internet, with devastating results. Cybercriminals were also able to reach out and con people from a distance with phishing attacks. No longer was it necessary to engage with individuals directly. You could attempt to trick millions of users simultaneously. Even if only a small percentage of people took the bait you stood to make a lot of money as a cybercriminal.

The 2000s brought us social media and saw the rise of identity theft. A bullseye was painted for cybercriminals with the creation of databases containing millions of users' **personal identifiable information (PII)**, making identity theft the new financial piggy bank for criminal organizations around the world.

This information coupled with a lack of cybersecurity awareness from the general public allowed cybercriminals to commit all types of financial fraud such as opening bank accounts and credit cards in the name of others.

Today we see that cybercriminal activity has only gotten worse. As computer systems have gotten faster and more complex we see that the cybercriminal has become more sophisticated and harder to catch. Today we have botnets, which are a network of private computers that are infected with malicious software and allow the criminal element to control millions of infected computer systems across the globe. These botnets allow the criminal element to overload organizational networks and hide the origin of the criminals:

- We see constant ransomware attacks across all sectors of the economy
- People are constantly on the lookout for identity theft and financial fraud
- Continuous news reports regarding the latest point of sale attack against major retailers and hospitality organizations

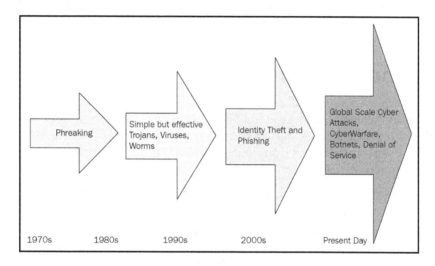

The modern role of information security

The role that information security plays has changed over the years and today, with information security professionals being brought in at the executive level of organizations, they have become critical members that contribute to the overall success of business operations. When information security first became a discipline, its focus was all about securing IT configurations and putting security tools in place. As time has progressed, it became apparent that you cannot properly secure an IT environment without first understanding the needs of an organization's business leaders. Now, information security leaders work to ensure that the business maintains its ability to serve its customers by tying cybersecurity to the business' functions.

IT security engineering

IT security engineering is the application of security principles to information technology. In our modern world, this really can mean just about anything, from a server to a refrigerator, once you start to consider the **Internet of Things** (**IoT**). There are so many new devices being built daily that are IP addressable, essentially making them mini-servers, which introduces potential vulnerabilities. Additionally, it is important to consider the security needs for devices that are non-networked or may be air gapped. Nonnetworked, or air-gapped, environments still have the capability to communicate through out-of-band means, such as a USB thumb drive, allowing an attacker to communicate with them. A mature organization should have staff specifically targeted at looking at information technology security concerns, working with business and information technology leadership to secure IT systems and protect the environment from attackers.

Information assurance

Information assurance is the act of working with business and IT leadership to ensure that the confidentiality, integrity, and availability requirements for a given asset are fully understood. Those requirements should be fully tested in a test environment prior to being integrated into the production environment, in order to ensure that they are secure and do not cause interoperability issues.

The activities associated with information assurance inform the activities associated with IT security regarding the specific technical controls needed to properly protect a given asset. Requirements are driven by the business/mission owner.

For example, a medical device might be deemed by a business/mission owner to be confidentiality-high, integrity-high, and availability-moderate (because they can revert to old school medical techniques):

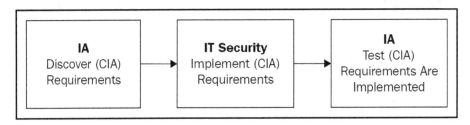

Relationship between Information Assurance and IT Security

The CIA triad

The CIA triad is a key tenet at the core of information security. This tool is used to help the information security professional think about how to best protect organizational data:

- **Confidentiality**: It has to do with whether or not information is kept secret or private. Mechanisms should be employed, such as encryption, which will render the data useless if it was accessed in an unauthorized manner.
- **Integrity**: It has to do with whether the information is kept accurate. Information should not be modified in an unauthorized manner and safeguards should be put in place that allows for detectable and timely unauthorized changes.
- **Availability**: It has to do with ensuring that information is available when it is needed. This control can be accomplished by implementing tools ranging from battery backup at the data center, to a content distribution network in the cloud:

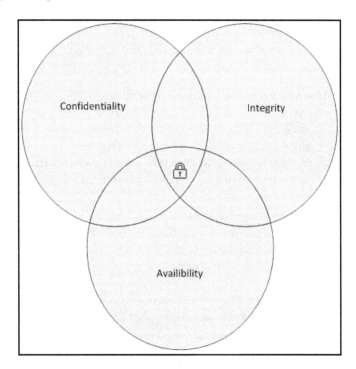

Organizational information security assessment

We must remember that information security is meant to compliment the business/mission process, and that each process owner will have to determine what risk is acceptable for their organization. We, as information security experts, can only offer recommendations (fixes, mitigations, and so on), but the business/mission owner is ultimately the individual who makes such decisions.

It is important to understand that in most cases, organizations must share information in today's digital economy in order to be successful. The key to a successful information security program is to properly categorize data and ensure that only those that are authorized to access the data have the rights to do so. This means that you need to look at data and your organization's staff members, business partners, vendors, and customers, and determine who should have access to the various types of data within your organization.

There are two main ways to conduct an assessment of your organization's IT and business process as they relate to information security:

- **Internal assessment**: An internal assessment can be viewed in two ways:
    - An initial assessment could be used to provide the context for the inclusion of a third-party assessment. This would be an appropriate course of action if your information security program lacked the skills to conduct a thorough information security assessment, or your organization prefers third-party assessments over internal assessments.
    - If your organization does not require a third-party assessment, and if you have the resources and skills to complete an information security assessment, the internal information security program can conduct its own assessment.

- **Third-party assessment**: The third-party assessment can be viewed in two ways:
    - A third-party assessment provides an objective view and can often be used to arbitrate between the information security group and IT operations. The third party brings in an unbiased observer to develop the organization's assessment, alleviating internal infighting.
    - While this has benefits over an initial assessment, this is usually the only mechanism for an assessment that is tied to compliance.

Recommendation

In my experience, the best way to start your information security program is to take a hybrid approach to conducting your initial assessment.

The following is an abbreviated example to begin the process of performing an internal assessment:

1. Conduct an initial internal assessment:
    1. As an information security leader you need to understand the organization you work in:
        1. Meet with business and IT leaders:
            1. Depending on the business function of your organization, acquire all past audit (PCI, HIPPA, and so on) reports, to determine what was found, addressed, not addressed, and so on.
        2. Meet with subject matter experts.
        3. Document areas for improvement and places where you can celebrate current successes.
        4. Brief leadership on your findings.
    2. Based on your findings recommend to leadership that a third party be brought in to dig deeper:
        1. No matter the results of the internal review, a third-party validator should be brought in, at least on a biannual basis to test your security program. This includes:
            1. Information security program reviews.
            2. Red team penetration test capability.
2. Conduct a third-party assessment:
    1. Work with IT leadership and subject matter experts to discuss the purpose of the assessment:
        1. Make sure that the assessment is **non-punitive**:
            1. Ensure that everyone understands that you are conducting an assessment to build a plan and roadmap. The purpose is not to fire individuals or to point out mistakes.
    2. Ensure that the third-party assessment has management buy-in and support:
        1. Without top-level support (Board, CEO), it might be easy for individuals to ignore your assessors.

   3. Ensure that the third party has access to the internal resources required:

      1. Make sure that there is a clear plan and that this plan is communicated to everyone that will be involved in the assessment.

   4. Conduct the assessment and produce the findings.

   5. A plan of action and milestones should then be developed with each business owner, to allow those owners to build their strategies of risk management, risk acceptance, or risk transfer.

Risk management

After having conducted a security assessment of the organization it will then become necessary to take your security assessment data and conduct a risk assessment. In conducting a risk assessment you can begin to prioritize the activities that you want to implement first, second, and so on, as you build your security program. During the risk assessment, you will want to take what you learned from the organization's leaders and ensure your prioritization serves the organization's goals so that you effectively describe your assessment and plan in business terms. Ultimately, the introduction of an information security program is one of organizational change. You want to ensure that you are presenting the changes you wish to make in organizational terms versus IT terms. This will help you to win the approval of leadership, which will provide you with the needed authority and funding to make changes to the organization.

Managing an information security program is really about risk management. Ultimately, how an organization deals with specific vulnerabilities in its IT systems, business processes, and staff has to do with its ability to manage risk. Organizational leaders are going to want to understand how vulnerabilities found in the assessment are going to impact the organization's ability to conduct business or serve their customers. Leadership will also want to understand the likelihood of a risk occurring and what the potential impact could be if this occurred.

It is important to identify the possible business impact of the risk. Each business owner will have its own risk concerns, and each business risk will be tied to a business function/dollar amount. Recommendations for fixes, mitigations, and so on, should tie into the **return on investment (ROI)**. For example:

- A HIPPA violation could cost an organization millions, however, a solution to the risk might only cost $38,000 annually, which will mitigate the risk and lower the overall risk posture.
- If you break that $38,000 down by the number of users who have access to the data, say 11,000, you come down to $3.45 per user for minimizing the risk posture. Your return on investment is easy to argue, and gain leadership support for.

Armed with this information, you can build out a plan that describes the specific IT implementations that need to be carried out in an organization based on the assessments that were previously conducted and the risk assessment that followed. The plan contains the priorities identified in the risk assessment process.

Based on the risk assessment, you will know the following:

- What the top risks are in the organization
- What the most valuable assets are for your organization
- What risks are most likely to occur
- What the impacts will be when a risk occurs

With this information, you have everything necessary to build a well-supported evidence-based plan to move your organization forward as it changes to implement modern information security practices.

Information security standards

Information security standards are published works by various professional organizations which attempt to encapsulate the guidance necessary to properly secure an IT system. Different standards have applicability to different industries, such as payment card versus healthcare, but tend to cover the full breadth of applicable system-related components, such as network devices, workstations, servers, software, user interaction with systems, system process interactions, data transmission, and storage. It is very important to understand that information security standards are not checklists.

When implementing a security standard for your organization you must look at the standard and decide how you will implement it for you organization. In most cases, the standard information is not prescriptive in that it does not tell you what tools to implement and how to implement them. You need to work with your IT and business teams to determine the best tools for the job and how they should be implemented within your infrastructure. It is also important to note that implementing a standard does not mean that you have effectively secured your organization. This is the trap of thinking of a standard as a checklist. You must look at an information security standard as a place to start. It is up to the information security professional to implement a standard in an effective way that properly secures the organization and mitigates risk to acceptable levels.

The following are some popular standards that are used around the globe:

- ISO 27001 and 27002
  (`https://www.iso.org/isoiec-27001-information-security.html`):
    - A set of requirements which provide a framework for an organization to plan, and assess their security.
    - It has a very specific mechanism. An organization can contract a third party to verify their security controls and so be deemed compliant with 27001.
- Voluntary NIST Cybersecurity Framework
  (`https://www.nist.gov/cyberframework`):
    - Guidance developed to help private sector entities and critical infrastructure develop an effective risk-based approach to implementing cybersecurity.
    - Provides information security activities, outcomes, references, and detailed guidance necessary for planning a well-functioning information security program.
    - Voluntary.
- HIPPA (`https://www.hhs.gov/hipaa/`):
    - The **Health Insurance Portability and Accountability Act** of 1996 (**HIPAA**) required the secretary of the U.S. department of **Health and Human Services** (**HHS**) to develop regulations protecting the privacy and security of certain health information.

- To fulfill this requirement, HHS published what is commonly known as the *HIPAA Privacy Rule* and the *HIPAA Security Rule*. The Privacy Rule, or standards for privacy of individually identifiable health information, establishes national standards for the protection of certain health information. The security standards for the protection of electronic protected health information (the Security Rule) establish a national set of security standards for protecting certain health information that is held or transferred in electronic form.
  - Mandatory requirement for any organization processing HIPPA-related data (**Personal Health Information (PHI)**).
- PCI DSS (`https://www.pcisecuritystandards.org/`):
  - The PCI **Data Security Standard (DSS)** provides a framework for developing a payment card data security process, which includes prevention, detection, and incident response to security incidents.
  - Mandatory requirement for any organization processing payment card data.

Policies

A policy is a foundational aspect to the development of a strong information security program. When developing a policy, you should ensure that you follow a few key principles:

- Receive board-level / CEO approval and support:
  - Without CEO or board-level backing, a security program is doomed to fail
- You should only create a policy that you intend to follow:
  - This means do not create a policy for the sake of the documentation. A policy that sits on the shelf and is never used does not help anyone.
  - Policies that you don't follow will be used by an auditor to show that you are deficient:
    - If you have policies follow them.

- Ensure your policies are implementable:
    - There are many ways that a security standard can be met, and your policies should reflect the way that your organization wants to implement a standard
    - Do not describe four points in a policy if you intend to only implement two of them if those two provide adequate risk mitigation
- A policy needs to take into account the organization's appetite for accepting risk:
    - Consider the value of the information that your organization owns.
    - Consider what would happen to the organization if you lost control over the *confidentiality*, *integrity*, and/or *availability* of the information:
        - Are you trying to safeguard trade secrets or sensitive proprietary information (confidentiality)?
        - Does information need to be accurate at all times (integrity)?
        - Could the organization effectively operate without its information (availability)?
    - Answers to questions like these, combined with an understanding of you organizations risk appetite, will inform your policy development.

Training

In our modern era, human interaction is a key vector used to exploit an information system. Whether you are looking at attacks such as ransomware, or exploits against critical infrastructure, the easiest avenue into a system is by tricking the user to run a piece of software. The key way that we can make sure that our users are prepared for these attacks is by implementing an effective training and awareness program.

Key components of an effective training and awareness program

An effective training and awareness program is necessary to ensure successful implementation of your information security program. A training and awareness program will be the primary mechanism used to communicate organizational user roles and responsibilities from an information security perspective:

- Secondary media products:
    - This includes things like giveaways (squeezy balls), alert notifications, posters, or social media.
    - These serve to remind users about information security principles that you are communicating through other mechanisms.
    - The key here is to keep information brief and manageable. If you need to read for more than ten seconds, it is too long.

- Primary media products:
    - This includes things such as email newsletters, websites, and inclusions in corporate magazines.
    - These have more contact and are distributed on a periodic basis.
    - The key here is to not overwhelm the user. If you send out an email newsletter every week, you may find your newsletter in the spam folder.

- Yearly information security awareness training:
    - This is training provided every year, where you communicate all of your information security requirements for the user into a single presentation
    - The preferred method for implementing this training is computer-based, through a learning management system:
        - This helps you to easily record users that have completed training and their scores
    - This training should include a mechanism to test the users' understanding:
        - The test should **not** be an information security vocabulary test:
            - The user should know not to click on URLs and attachments they do not trust

- The user does not need to be test on the difference between phishing or spear phishing
- Use the yearly training as an opportunity to have your users validate or revalidate their acceptance of your organization's acceptable use policy:
  - The training should cover every aspect of the Acceptable Use Policy

- Events:
  - This includes lunch time presentations, webinars, and presenting at corporate, divisional, or team meetings
  - It is very important to deliver the information security message to your organization in person where possible:
    - Webinars are useful in geographically-distributed organizations
  - Getting 15 minutes to speak at the finance or HR teams quarterly meeting is a great way to answer questions that an entire group may have

For example, payroll and benefit processors may have questions on PII handling and protections.

References:

- More information on the ISO 27001 standard is available at: `https://www.iso.org/isoiec-27001-information-security.html`
- More information on NIST Cybersecurity Framework is available at: `https://www.nist.gov/cyberframework`
- More information on the Health Insurance Portability and Accountability Act is available at: `https://www.hhs.gov/hipaa/`
- More information on the Payment Card Industry Data Security Standard is available at: `https://www.pcisecuritystandards.org/`

Summary

In this chapter, we covered introductory topics on implementing an effective information security program. We discussed the following:

- Information security challenges faced by the organization and the information security program
- The evolution of cybercrime over time and its impact
- The role of information security in the organization
- The concept of confidentiality, integrity, and availability
- An introduction to information security assessments
- An introduction to risk management
- The roles of information security standards and training
- How awareness and training benefit the organization

In the next chapter, we will define the threat landscape. We will be discussing the people, processes, and technologies that need to be defended against to ensure your organization's continued security.

Defining the Threat Landscape

2

Understanding the modern threat landscape will help you as an information security professional in developing a highly effective information security program that can mount a secure defense against modern adversaries in support of your organization's business/mission goals and objectives.

In this chapter, you will learn:

- How to determine what is important to your organization
- Potential threats to your organization
- Types of hackers/adversaries
- Methods used by the hacker/adversary
- Methods of conducting training and awareness as it relates to threats

What is important to your organization and who wants it?

It is important to understand what is important to your organization in order to properly protect the organization from potential threats. The information security professional must look beyond just information technology and take a look at the organization they work for and understand its concerns.

The information security professional must understand documents such as the corporate mission and vision statements. These documents answer questions such as:

- What does the organization do?
    - Do you make car tires, or do you provide services to the elderly?
- Who are the organization's customers?
    - Who receives your services?
- Who is the organization?
    - What is the organizational culture? How does the organization want to be viewed?
    - Who are your third-party partners within your business structure?
        - Use Target, Home Depot, and now Equifax as examples, where access to the organizations' information systems was achieved through third-party vendors

Answers to questions such as these can help the information security professional to understand what it is they are trying to protect. Understanding the business of your organization will help you better understand who may be interested in getting access to your intellectual property or to the information that you may serve as the custodian.

Taking this a step further, it is important for the information security professional to reach out to and work with all levels of management within the organization. In reaching out to the functional mission-driven parts of the organization, you will begin to understand how these groups are taking the organization mission and vision and applying it to their day-to-day work.

It is at this point where you begin to understand where trade secrets and intellectual property exist and what the impact would be to the organization if this information was:

- **C**: Provided to a competitor
- **I**: Altered
- **A**: Destroyed

While you are working with mission-focused groups within the organization, it is very important to present yourself as a person that can help complement a business need as it relates to protecting their information and helping them to continue doing business. When you are working to identify business-critical information, you should not be discussing technology. You should be focusing on business functions and the important data within those business functions:

- If you discuss financial concerns with finance, you will find allies
- If you discuss IT security with finance, you will be ignored

Compliance

Once you have established mission-focused relationships within your organization and have identified the highly sensitive information that the organization uses to operate, you should begin to analyze this information as it relates to organizational compliance requirements and your knowledge of the threats that the organization faces.

If your organization is responsible for oil refining, you may have a very different response to securing an information system than you would if you were a hospital and you were looking to secure a network-connected blood pressure machine.

References:

- **Financial (FFIEC-IT)**: https://ithandbook.ffiec.gov/it-booklets/e-banking/ risk-management-of-e-banking-activities/information-security-program/ security-guidelines.aspx
- **Retail (PCI-DSS)**: https://www.pcisecuritystandards.org/document_library
- **HealthCare (HIPAA)**: https://www.hhs.gov/hipaa/for-professionals/index. html
- **Defence (DFARS)**: http://www.acq.osd.mil/dpap/dars/dfarspgi/current/
- **Energy (CIP)**: http://www.nerc.com/pa/Stand/Pages/CIPStandards.aspx

Hackers and hacking

We can start the conversation around who wants your information by first beginning to define the hacker. A hacker is someone who has the knowledge and skills necessary to circumvent the security controls or detect and exploit vulnerabilities in an information system.

Black hat hacker

A black hat hacker is an individual who compromises a computer system with malicious intent and without the permission of the owner of the information system. These individuals are engaged in criminal activities and are the ones that are behind the technical implementation and proliferation of cybercrime that we have seen grow across the world. The term black hat hacker was pulled from western films where the criminal in the movie would wear a black hat.

White hat or ethical hacker

A white hat or ethical hacker is a person that uses their knowledge and skills to circumvent a computer system's security controls with the knowledge of an information system owner. White hat hackers typically present themselves from a services point of view as a penetration tester who performs penetration tests on information systems.

Blue hat hacker

A blue hat hacker is very much like a white hat hacker. These information security professionals are invited by vendors to test their products. This is often conducted in the form of software bug testing prior to a product launch or version release.

Grey hat hacker

A grey hat hacker is someone who sits in between the two types of hackers. The grey hat hacker will often hack into a system with the intention of notifying the information system owner of the weakness. The grey hat does not have permission to attack the information system in this case, and is often performing this service with an expectation of being paid to disclose the vulnerability to the information system owner. Other grey hat hackers will publish their findings to the internet. In some cases, they are doing this to showcase their capabilities. In other cases, they do this to disclose a flaw in order to force a vendor to fix the software package. It is important to note that hacking without an information system owner's permission is illegal.

Penetration testing

The penetration test is an authorized attack against an information system which is used to simulate a real attack that could be perpetrated by a black hat hacker.

Penetration testing is a very important part of the information security program and is needed in order to find hidden vulnerabilities in the information system. Many organizations implement vulnerability assessment tools but do not add penetration testing to their overall testing methodology. Penetration testing is important because it allows the information security program to uncover vulnerabilities that are not easily captured through automated means. The penetration tester takes their information security knowledge and uses it to systematically break into an information system even when a vulnerability scanner has not found a vulnerability present.

Remember that there are various levels of penetration testing:

- Those that are fully engaged and coordinated with your business and its operations personnel
- To red team penetration testing, which is the same as a black hat

Also, remember that penetration testing covers a full array of activities that include:

- Physical security test
- Network intrusions
- Social engineering, and so on

A penetration testing engagement from a white hat / ethical hacker can include services such as:

- Collecting trash from trash cans and dumpsters in order to look for passwords and intellectual property
- Pretending to be the organization's helpdesk in an attempt to retrieve user passwords
- Social engineering attacks such as phishing and spear phishing attacks
- Web-based application attacks
- Vulnerability scanning
- Port scanning and so on

Hacktivist

A hacktivist is very much like a black hat hacker. These individuals use their computer security knowledge to attack organizations with the purpose of making a political or social change.

Script kiddie

A script kiddie is not a skilled hacker, but rather someone that has used automated hacking tools to attack information systems. These individuals use scripts and tools developed by other highly skilled hackers to perform their attacks. Because script kiddies lack the knowledge, they tend to cause unintended damage as they don't fully understand the tools they are using. Also, their lack of knowledge makes them much easier for law enforcement to apprehend. Experienced hackers understand how to go mostly undetected and can cover their tracks. Script kiddies don't have this skill and leave a large trail leading back to them.

Nation state

A nation state attacker is an attacker that is sponsored by the government of a country. These types of adversaries are highly skilled and have immense resources at their disposal. Nation state activities can best be described in terms of cyber warfare where the nation state actor is motivated to engage in espionage and/or sabotage against another country. The nation states' motivations include military targets, national critical infrastructure, acts of political hacktivism, terrorism, and private sector or non-profit intellectual property.

Cybercrime

Cybercrime is a crime that involves the use of a computer. The computer may have been the target of a cybercrime or it could have been used to conduct a cybercrime. In 2014, a report sponsored by McAfee estimated that cybercrime had damaged the world economy by 445 billion dollars. Cybercrime can be committed by organized criminal gangs as well as individuals that have procured the necessary tools:

- **Fraud and financial crimes**: Fraud is a misrepresentation of fact that is intended to manipulate another into doing or not doing an act that causes a financial loss:
    - Fraud can result by the altering, suppressing/destroying, or exfiltration of electronic data
    - Forms of computer fraud include identity theft, extortion, and bank fraud

- **Cyber extortion**: This occurs when an organization is subjected, by electronic means, to repeated attacks whereby the attacker demands money to stop the attacks:
    - Forms of cyber extortion include denial of service and ransomware attacks
    - The insider threat

Methods used by the attacker

Here, we will explore the methods used by an attacker to exploit and gain access or control of enterprise information systems.

Exploits

Attackers utilize exploits to gain unauthorized access to an information system. An exploit takes advantage of vulnerabilities in an information system by implementing custom software, operating system commands, and open source tools.

The most pervasive and destructive web application vulnerabilities are cataloged and well defined by the **Open Web Application Security Project** (**OWASP**). This organization has maintained a top 10 list for many years where they provide the tools to understand web application exploits and provide the information necessary for the developer to fix these issues in their applications. The OWASP website should be visited as it contains a wealth of information that can be used to enhance the security of your information and application security programs.

 For more information on OWASP, please refer to `https://www.owasp.org/index.php/Category:OWASP_Top_Ten_Project`.

The OWASP top 10 vulnerabilities for 2017 are as follows:

- **Injection**: Injection flaws, such as SQL, OS, XXE, and LDAP injection occur when untrusted data is sent to an interpreter as part of a command or query. The attacker's hostile data can trick the interpreter into executing unintended commands or accessing data without proper authorization.

- **Broken authentication and session management**: Application functions related to authentication and session management are often implemented incorrectly, allowing attackers to compromise passwords, keys, or session tokens, or to exploit other implementation flaws to assume other users' identities (temporarily or permanently).
- **Cross-site scripting (XSS)**: XSS flaws occur whenever an application includes untrusted data in a new web page without proper validation or escaping, or updates an existing web page with user-supplied data using a browser API that can create JavaScript. XSS allows attackers to execute scripts in the victim's browser that can hijack user sessions, deface websites, or redirect the user to malicious sites.
- **Broken access control**: Restrictions on what authenticated users are allowed to do are not properly enforced. Attackers can exploit these flaws to access unauthorized functionality and/or data, such as access other users' accounts, view sensitive files, modify other users' data, change access rights, and so on.
- **Security misconfiguration**: Good security requires having a secure configuration defined and deployed for the application, frameworks, application server, web server, database server, platform, and so on. Secure settings should be defined, implemented, and maintained, as defaults are often insecure. Additionally, software should be kept up to date.
- **Sensitive data exposure**: Many web applications and APIs do not properly protect sensitive data, such as financial, healthcare, and PII. Attackers may steal or modify such weakly protected data to conduct credit card fraud, identity theft, or other crimes. Sensitive data deserves extra protection such as encryption at rest or in transit, as well as special precautions when exchanged with the browser.
- **Insufficient attack protection**: The majority of applications and APIs lack the basic ability to detect, prevent, and respond to both manual and automated attacks. Attack protection goes far beyond basic input validation and involves automatically detecting, logging, responding, and even blocking exploit attempts. Application owners also need to be able to deploy patches quickly to protect against attacks.
- **Cross-Site Request Forgery**: A CSRF attack forces a logged-on victim's browser to send a forged HTTP request, including the victim's session cookie and any other automatically included authentication information, to a vulnerable web application. Such an attack allows the attacker to force a victim's browser to generate requests the vulnerable application thinks are legitimate requests from the victim.

- **Using components with known vulnerabilities**: Components such as libraries, frameworks, and other software modules run with the same privileges as the application. If a vulnerable component is exploited, such an attack can facilitate serious data loss or server takeover. Applications and APIs using components with known vulnerabilities may undermine application defenses and enable various attacks and impacts.
- **Unprotected APIs**: Modern applications often involve rich client applications and APIs, such as JavaScript in the browser and mobile apps, that connect to an API of some kind (SOAP/XML, REST/JSON, RPC, GWT, and so on). These APIs are often unprotected and contain numerous vulnerabilities.

Hacker techniques

We will now take a look at some of the techniques and tools used by the attacker to launch their attacks and campaigns:

- **Password cracking**: The hacker utilizes specialized software to recover passwords that have been transmitted over the network, from recovered password databases stored at rest, and application software that implements their own methods of authentication. A common method for implementing password cracking is to implement automated guessing through the use of password dictionaries.

  The following is a list of the password cracking tools that we can use:
  - **Brutus**: http://sectools.org/tool/brutus/
  - **RainbowCrack**: http://sectools.org/tool/rainbowcrack/
  - **Wfuzz**: http://sectools.org/tool/wfuzz/
  - **Cain and Abel**: http://sectools.org/tool/cain/
  - **John the Ripper**: http://sectools.org/tool/john/
  - **THC Hydra**: http://sectools.org/tool/hydra/
  - **Medusa**: http://sectools.org/tool/medusa/
  - **ophcrack**: http://sectools.org/tool/ophcrack/
  - **L0phtCrack**: http://sectools.org/tool/l0phtcrack/
  - **Aircrack-ng**: https://www.aircrack-ng.org/downloads.html

- **Vulnerability assessment scanner tools**: These tools utilize databases of known vulnerabilities with specialized software that scan the network to see if there are any matches with the database. The tool then creates a vulnerability listing that ties the vulnerability to an IP address so that it can be reviewed. In the case of an administrator, this list can be used to fix an information system. In the case of an attacker, this list is the front door.

  The following is a list of the vulnerability assessment scanner tools that we can use:

  - **OpenVAS**: http://www.openvas.org/
  - **Burp Suite**: https://portswigger.net/burp/communitydownload
  - **Arachni**: http://www.arachni-scanner.com/
  - **w3af**: http://w3af.org/
  - **Vega**: https://subgraph.com/vega/
  - **Nmap**: https://nmap.org/
  - **Microsoft Baseline Security Analyze**: https://www.microsoft.com/en-us/download/details.aspx?id=7558
  - **Qualys FreeScan**: https://www.qualys.com/forms/freescan/
  - **Nessus**: https://www.tenable.com/products/nessus-home
  - **Rapid7 (InsightVM and Metasploit)**: https://www.rapid7.com/

- **Manual vulnerability assessment**: The truly skilled hacker is able to test information systems based on their own knowledge for vulnerabilities that scanners cannot detect. This is where manual testing comes into play.

Manual testing also clearly marks the division between vulnerability assessment and penetration testing as part of the information security program. In order to have an effective program, you must ensure that your periodic testing includes manual/penetration testing. Without this type of testing, you will be missing the information system's vulnerabilities that your adversaries won't miss.

- **Keystroke logging**: With keystroke logging, the attacker installs either software or a physical device on the computer with the intention of capturing all keystrokes entered on the computer:
  - **Software-based keyloggers**: Following are the hypervisor-based keyloggers:
    - **Hypervisor-based keyloggers**: It operates at the hypervisor level of a virtualized infrastructure and sits at a place below the operating system. In this case, known detection tools at the operating system level will be able to detect the keylogger.

- **Kernel-based keyloggers**: It operates in the kernel mode of the operating system as a rootkit and is typically not detectable by antivirus tools as they do not have access to the layer of the operating system.

- **Hardware-based keyloggers**: Following are the hardware-based keyloggers:
    - **Keyboard hardware**: These types of keyloggers are connected between a computer and a keyboard. They contain internal memory and intercept keystrokes sent from the keyboard to the computer. This type of keylogger requires physical access to the computer.

- **Wireless keyboard sniffers**: Specialized hardware and software that can intercept keystrokes sent between a wireless keyboard and the computer it is attached to. This type of keylogger requires that the attacker is in close proximity to the computer being attacked.

- **Rootkit**: A rootkit is a piece of software that is installed by a hacker that is very difficult to detect and is used to take control of an operating system. A rootkit replaces key operating system software causing the operating system to appear normal when in fact it contains malware. Because rootkits run at such low levels in the operating system, they have the ability to make themselves look legitimate by responding to higher levels in the operating system with information that is expected as part of normal operations:

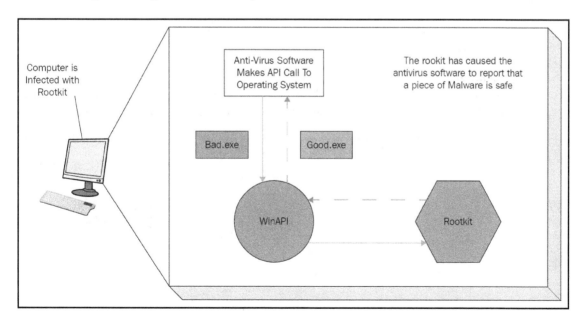

- **Spoofing**: As part of a spoofing attack, a hacker will install software or build a system with the intention of mimicking another system. In some cases, the hacker may spoof themselves with the intention of appearing like a trusted client system in order to gain access to a backend server environment. In other cases, the hacker will spoof themselves as the underlying information system infrastructure in order to harvest information from unsuspecting users. Hackers can use this technique to harvest sensitive company information and passwords to backend information systems:

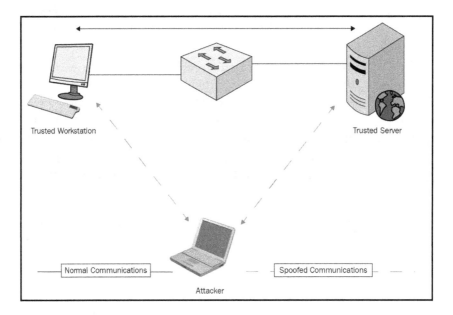

- **Social engineering**: This hacking technique is very hands-on and can often not include any special tools other than the hacker. Social engineering has to do with manipulating an individual's natural bias to want to trust another person:

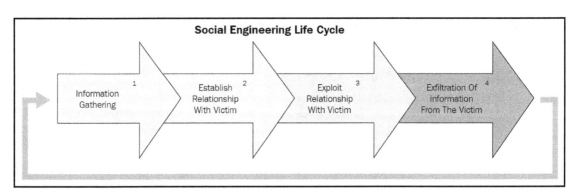

- **Pretexting**: With pretexting, the hacker creates a scenario that they use against their victim to lure them into divulging information that will allow the attacker to gain further access to the organization's information system. As part of the scenario, an attacker will establish a position of authority so that the user believes that the request is valid, and that the attacker has a right to know their confidential information.

  An example of pretexting is when a hacker contacts a user of a company posing as a member of the organization's information technology team. They can make a request for the user to provide them with their username and password so that they can troubleshoot an issue with an information system. In many cases, a user will hand over their credentials because they believe that the individual requesting the username and password are well-intentioned and want to do a service for the user. In reality, the hacker has just harvested the user credentials and will use them to further their intrusion into the information system.

- **Phishing**: Using these techniques, hackers can take the concept of pretexting and apply some technology to expand the number of individuals they are reaching at a single moment. In the pretexting example, the attacker was reaching out to a single user at a time. With the phishing example, the attacker can reach millions of users in a single campaign.

  An example of phishing is receiving an email saying that your bank information is no longer valid and that you need to log in to your bank's website to fix the issue. In the case of a well-executed phishing campaign:
    - The email will contain a link for you to click that will take you to the attacker's website rather than the actual bank's website.
    - The attacker's website will look and function like the bank's website.
    - The URL in the browser will look similar to the URL of the bank's website.
    - The attacker's website will accept the user credentials and pass the user to the real website. The user will not realize that anything has happened.

The following screenshot is an example of a phishing campaign. Notice that the email appears to come from Netflix and that it generically addresses the user. The link will take the user to the attacker's website if clicked. This image is taken from an actual phishing message:

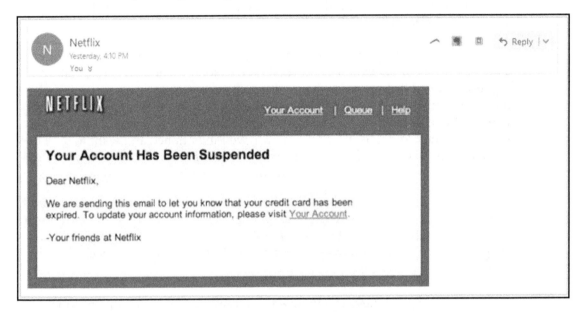

- **Spear phishing**: While very similar to phishing, spear phishing adds a dimension of analysis on the part of the attacker against the victim. With spear phishing, the attacker performs reconnaissance against their victim in order to gain important personal details that the victim will recognize as information that only a colleague would have. Therefore, the main difference between phishing and spear phishing is that the attacker sends a customized email to lure a single user, versus the millions of emails that are sent out in a phishing campaign. The success of spear phishing attacks is higher than phishing attacks because of the customization that goes into the spear phishing email.

- **Water holing**: This attack takes advantage of websites that contain vulnerabilities and that a user trusts. In this attack, the adversary will do reconnaissance to determine websites that a user or group of users often use within an organization. The attacker will then work to compromise the trusted website. Once the website is compromised, the website can be used as a platform to install malware on the unsuspecting users' machines. The attacker can simply wait for the users to go to the website or they can craft a spear phishing email to lure them to the site.

- **Baiting**: In baiting, the attacker will use a physical medium such as DVDs and USB drives to trick the users into placing the drives into their computers. In practice, it doesn't really take a whole lot of tricking as users will often insert removable media they have no reason to trust in their computers. As with phishing, the best defense against baiting is training the users ahead of time:

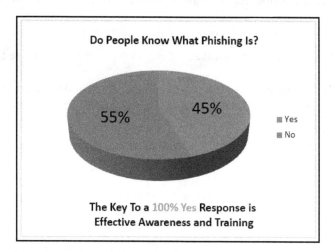

- **Awareness training to combat phishing**: The most effective countermeasure you can put in place to combat phishing is to raise the awareness of your user population to the threat of phishing and spear phishing. It is easy for the information security professional to become complacent and believe that everyone knows about phishing and that there is no reason to waste time with a training program. However, this couldn't be further from the truth. As information security professionals, we must remember that other parts of the organization exist to perform their specialized work and they do not exist to ponder interesting facts about information security. Other members of the organization sitting in their various departments (HR, finance, manufacturing, and so on) will be surprised to find out that others outside of the organization may want to contact them for the purpose of using them to commit fraud against the organization.

Methods of conducting training and awareness

As we begin to think about training and awareness, we need to compile the methods we intend on using to conduct outreach:

- Include specific phishing training as part of your yearly information security training:
    - If you don't conduct yearly training, start
- Develop a cycle for communicating with your entire user base through an email newsletter:
    - Develop a plan where a certain number of these newsletters are used to deliver targeted phishing awareness training
- Conduct phishing exercises:
    - Utilize automated tools that allow you to test your user base for their awareness of phishing threats. These tools should allow you to:
        - Import your user population from your user directory instead of manually inputting them into the tool
        - Should allow you to build multiple campaigns so that you can target different user groups at the same time
        - The tools should allow you to track users that get exploited as part of the training so that they can be scheduled for additional training

Users should not be treated negatively if they are determined to need additional training. The process should be positive, and the users should feel that they are learning a new skill instead of feeling that they are being reprimanded.

Closing information system vulnerabilities

As it relates to information security, a vulnerability is a weakness in a piece of technology (workstation, server, router, IOT, software, cloud, and so on), or a process (operational or management) that lessens the ability to provide assurance that the information system is secure.

In order to properly assess a vulnerability, three aspects of the vulnerability must be taken into account:

- Is the information system susceptible to a given flaw?
    - Millions of vulnerabilities exist. You must ascertain if your information system:
        - Meets the criteria where the vulnerability exists to include the specific version identified by the vendor
        - For example, version 1.01 of a piece of software may be vulnerable to an exploit, while version 1.02 is not

- Can an attacker access the information system in order to take advantage of the flaw?
    - Depending on the piece of technology, an attacker may not have ready access to information systems in order to exercise the vulnerability
    - This helps to inform the prioritization as it relates to enterprise vulnerability management (which vulnerabilities do you fix first?)
- Do sufficient means exist to exploit the flaw?
    - If an active exploit exists in the wild for a given vulnerability, high priority should be given to mitigate the vulnerability in the information system

Based on careful review of the characteristics of vulnerabilities as it relates to your specific information system, the information security professional will be able to ascertain the attack surface for a given vulnerability and establish a priority for how the enterprise should mitigate the vulnerability.

It is important to understand that at any given time hundreds of vulnerabilities could exist in an information system. The information security professional must be able to prioritize critical vulnerabilities that must be patched immediately (all hands on deck) versus vulnerabilities that could be planned out more methodically and mitigated in a much more reasoned approach.

Example triage chart for vulnerabilities	
All hands on deck	**Planned methodical deployment**
<ul><li>Vulnerability can be executed over the network</li><li>Information systems are internet exposed</li><li>Information system is not properly patched and is running old version of server software and/or operating system software</li></ul>	<ul><li>Vulnerability requires physical access to be exploited</li><li>Information system is well protected within the network</li><li>Server is well maintained and is properly patched</li></ul>

Vulnerability management

It is very important to note that many of the things that cause an all-hands-on-deck situation relate to how an enterprise information system is managed. If an enterprise information system is not regularly patched, then this leads to an all-hands-on-deck situation.

Vulnerability management is the process of:

- Identifying vulnerabilities that are applicable to your information system:
    - Vulnerabilities can be identified through the use of enterprise vulnerability management tools such as Nessus
    - Additionally, the information security professional should be reading information security blogs and should be subscribed to the security sites for the vendors that they use

- Triaging vulnerabilities that are applicable to your information system:
    - The information security professional must determine the risk that a given vulnerability presents to the organization and communicate that risk effectively
    - It must be clearly represented whether this is an all-hands-on-deck or a planned approach to the vulnerability mitigation exercise

- Researching, planning, and deploying mitigations to applicable vulnerabilities:
    - There may be multiple tasks that makeup vulnerability mitigation. The information security professional must fully understand these steps, effectively communicate these steps to stakeholders, and completely deploy the appropriate countermeasure to adequately mitigate the vulnerability.
- Monitoring the information systems to ensure that the vulnerabilities have been fully mitigated:
    - You must ensure that vulnerabilities have been fully mitigated within an information system
    - Utilizing a vulnerability assessment tool for this stage will allow you to continuously assess your information system during vulnerability mitigation to assess your progress and understand when you have met your goal

The case for vulnerability management

In June 2017, the Petya ransomware was a global threat that was taking advantage of an SMB flaw in the Windows operating system as a vector to propagate itself. For many enterprises, this became an all-hands-on-deck situation where systems were being patched in order to protect themselves from the ransomware. Microsoft released a patch for *CVE-2017-0199* in April 2017 that mitigated the flaw in the SMB protocol that Petya used. If enterprises had strong patch management procedures in place, the already released patch would have been deployed months before Petya became a global threat.

Summary

In this chapter, we covered the modern threat landscape so that we can better support:

- The development of our information security program
- Support business/mission goals and objectives
- Develop countermeasures that defend against modern threats

We discussed:

- How to determine what is important to your organization
- Potential threats to your organization
- Types of hackers/adversaries
- Methods used by the hacker/adversary
- Methods of conducting training and awareness as it relates to threats

In the next chapter, we will discuss the activities necessary to establish an enterprise-wide information security program focusing on policies, procedures, standards, and guidelines.

3
Preparing for Information and Data Security

In this chapter, we will be discussing the important activities required to establish an enterprise-wide information security program with a focus on executive buy-in, policies, procedures, standards, and guidelines.

In this chapter, you will learn:

- Planning concepts associated with the information security program establishment
- Information security program success factors
- SDLC integration of the information security program
- Information security program maturity concepts
- Policies, procedures, standards, and guidelines

Establishing an information security program

A top priority for any organization today should be the establishment and successful operation of an information security program. As you begin the planning for your information security program, you must take into account the unique aspects of your organization. Some of these aspects include:

- **Organization size**: The information security program for a small custom metal fabricator will be very different than for a car manufacturer.

- **Organization industry**: An organization that is focused on oil and gas exploration will have very different concerns than an organization that produces frozen TV dinners.
- **Organization compliance factors**: Do you process credit cards? Do your customers include governmental agencies? Are you publicly traded? Answers to these questions will affect the organization and operations of your information security program.

Don't start from scratch, use a framework

Do not start from scratch when you begin to establish your information security program. There are many excellent frameworks that exist that you can use to establish your information security program. Look to standards such as the ISO 27000 series, NIST Cybersecurity Framework, or COBIT 5. These organizations have collectively spent millions of dollars to establish these frameworks. Additionally, these frameworks have been peer-reviewed by thousands of subject matter experts. Your organization is not going to be able to bring these sorts of resources together in order to plan out a new framework. Take advantage of the previous work done by other great professionals and apply an existing framework within your organization.

Security program success factors

The key to the information security program's success is how well it integrates with the businesses objectives and culture. Additionally, it is very important that the information security program is well integrated into the various activities of the organization, ensuring that information security is always being considered.

Executive or board support

A key aspect of the success of your information security program is developing a strong relationship with your organization's senior leadership. Without the commitment from your organization's senior leadership, the information security program will most likely be ineffective. Information security is really about organizational change. When a new information security program is established within an organization, changes will occur across the spectrum of people, processes, and technology. These changes could potentially be seen as disruptive to the way things are normally done. Without strong executive support for the information security programs, it may be difficult to make the necessary changes.

It is important to note that executive support is not a license to cause havoc within your organization. It is still the job of the information security professional to work within all levels of the organization. You must communicate the need for information security in a way that clearly explains how the information security program is protecting the organization and how it is helping to allow the organization to continue serving its customers. In doing this, it is important to speak to the organizational team members.

Remember, the information security program's biggest challenge is changing the leadership and cultural views of the organization. You must have executive leader buy-in to be successful.

Supporting the organization's mission

As you are developing the information security program, it is critical that you work with your organization's senior management, business leaders, and system owners to determine what the needs are of your mission-focused entities. It is entirely possible that you could build a very secure information system that is completely useless to your business users if you do not include them in the process. You must have discussions about their mission activities, which will allow you to build a solution that allows those activities to continue in a secure manner.

Rightsizing information security for the organization

It is crucial to strike a balance between the implementation of security controls, the usability of an information system, and the risk appetite for an organization. The implementation of unnecessary security controls within an information system can lead to unnecessary complexity, a reduction in mission effectiveness, unnecessary financial expenditures, and ultimately a lack of confidence in the information security program.

Security awareness and training program

The information security training and awareness program is a key component of a successful information security program. Everyone in the organization, from the CEO to the newest person hired, has a role to play in ensuring that the organization stays secure. In order for an awareness and training program to be effective, the training must communicate the organization's expectations and threats that users may experience. An effective awareness and training program uses multiple media channels such as email, social media, and computer-based training to communicate the information security message.

Information security built into SDLC

An SDLC/SELC life cycle is used to ensure repeatable processes as part of an engineering and/or development project. An organization uses these processes to improve the predictability that a quality product will come out of the engineering or development process. The SDLC/SELC process, combined with strong security policies, will help to ensure a well-designed system that has security built in from project initiation. A typical SDLC/SELC process contains the following phases:

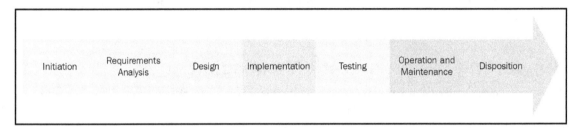

The following is the detailed explanation of different phases of SDLC/SELC:

- **Initiation phase**: During the initiation phase of a project, the organization defines the need for an information system. Information security planning begins in the initiation phase where the information security professional works with the project team to understand the security considerations that will need to be applied to the system.
- **Requirements analysis phase**: During the requirements analysis phase, the project team works with users and business stakeholders to develop the requirements necessary for the new system. It is the job of the information security professional to ensure that security requirements are included for the new system and that they are given a high priority.
- **Design phase**: During the design phase, the requirements that were gathered during the requirements analysis phase are used to construct the new system. The role of the information security professional in this phase is to ensure that the correct information security controls are implemented as part of the system design. The design phase can be further broken down into subphases where the engineering team develops:
  - **Concept of operation**: A document that describes the characteristics of a system from a user perspective. This document is used to communicate how the system will operate to business stakeholders.

- **High-level design**: A document that describes the logical components of a system and how they will interact. This document includes data flows and how part of the system will interconnect.
- **Detailed design**: A document that takes the high-level design and applies the specific configurations and costs that will be part of the system.
- **Proof of concept system**: A proof of concept system takes the detailed design and implements a system that can be used to determine if the design system meets the user and business stakeholder requirements. Often, the proof of concept is a scaled-down version of the proposed system in order to test functionality without incurring the full cost of the final system.

- **Implementation phase**: During the implementation phase, the project team builds the production information system based on the design defined in the previous phase. The role of the information security professional is to ensure that the designed security controls are properly implemented and working.
- **Testing phase**: During the testing phase, the project team executes an agreed upon test plan to ensure that the system functions as expected. The information security professional must ensure that the implemented security controls work as expected. If any deficiencies are discovered, the security control must be identified and flagged for repair.
- **Operations and maintenance phase**: During this phase, the system is in production and is under configuration management. The information security professional must ensure that any new changes to the system are thoroughly examined for their impact on the security controls that were applied during the implementation phase.
- **Disposition phase**: During the disposition phase, the useful life of the system has been reached and the business has decided to decommission the system. It is the responsibility of the information security professional to ensure that the system has been properly archived and sanitized in accordance with organizational policy and applicable laws.

Information security program maturity

As you work through the various frameworks, it is important to remember that they are not checklists. These frameworks need to be used to develop your own security program. A key aspect in developing a strong information security program is to understand that you should not be boiling the ocean. By this, I mean that you should not be trying to do so much that you end up doing nothing or worse, causing serious harm to the organization.

As you develop your plan to implement your information security program, you must consider where you are presently from an information security program maturity perspective. As you engage in planning, you need to think about how you can push your program along the maturity life cycle. As an example, you cannot push your organization into a place where you are implementing continuous and effective monitoring of security controls if you are implementing those controls in an ad hoc fashion. You must first focus on developing plans where information security control development is part of the organizational culture and system development life cycle.

- **Initial**:
    - No formal security program in place
    - Unstaffed or understaffed
    - Security controls are implemented in an ad hoc manner or not at all

- **Developing**:
    - Basic governance and risk management policies, standards, procedures, and guidelines are in place
    - Information security leadership is in place
    - Informal communications
    - Security controls begin to be developed and implemented

- **Defined**:
    - Information security roles such as system owner and data owner are defined
    - Organization-wide polices are in place with inadequate verification
    - More security controls are in place but lack automation

- **Managed**:
    - Clearly defined roles and responsibilities accompanied by role-based training
    - Formal information security communication with business stakeholders
    - Controls measured and monitored for compliance
    - Automation is still not fully used throughout the environment

- **Optimized**:
    - Culture of organization supports information security improvements for people, processes, and technology
    - Organization implements a risk-based management program for information security
    - Controls are comprehensively implemented across the environment

- Automation is implemented to support repeatable processes and continuous monitoring

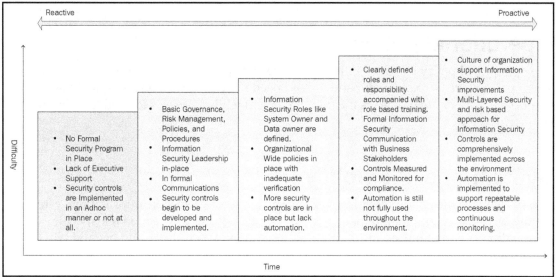

Information security policies

Information security policies establish the rules where organizations can direct funding, people, processes, and technology in a retable and secure manner. NIST SP 800-95, *Guide to Secure Web Services*, defines policy as:

"Statements, rules or assertions that specify the correct or expected behavior of an entity."

Information security policies are developed by examining compliance requirements, obligations under the law, and organization-wide policies and practices. These policies are responsible for establishing rules behind how an organization develops and operates systems utilizing their **system's engineering life cycle (SELC)** or **system's development life cycle (SDLC)**.

Information security program policy

As the name suggests, this type of policy establishes the organizational information security program. These policies set the strategic direction for the organization and assign specific resources and roles to establish and implement the information security program.

The information security program policy includes the program purpose, program scope, addresses compliance requirements, and assigns who is responsible for the information security program.

Operational policy

The operational policy provides guidance for specific policy areas at an organizational level. These policies are technology dependent and need to be reviewed on a frequent basis. Examples of operational policies include the recommended policies located later in this chapter.

System-specific policy

The system-specific policy provides guidance around how a specific information system should be operated and maintained. System-specific policies are needed if a specific information system requires additional policies and guidance above and beyond what the organizational policies cover:

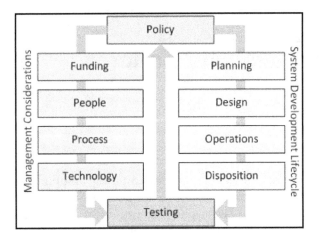

Standards

Information security standards are the quantifiable/measurable metrics that can be used to:

- Determine an organization's compliance with compliance standards or internal policies
- Determine whether or not a specific performance SLA is being met

An organization should use an already existing standard, such as those from NIST or ISO, rather than creating their own standards. The process of creating a standard is incredibly time-consuming. Tailoring an already existing standard to suit your organization's needs is a better option.

Procedures

Procedures are step-by-step mandatory guidance that is created in support of the policy. These documents help to ensure that repeatable/consistent processes exist to technically implement policy.

Procedures are designed to answer three questions:

- How should a particular activity be performed?
  - Account creation, password reset, or firewall rule change
- When should that activity be performed?
  - Hourly, daily, weekly, or monthly
- Who should perform the activity?
  - System administrator, network administrator, or incident responder

Guidelines

Guidelines are guidance provided to answer questions that may be encountered by organizational users. Guidelines can take the form of frequently asked questions or how-to manuals providing guidance to users within the organization:

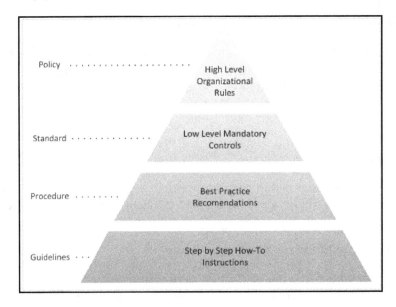

Recommended operational policies

Information security policies can be broken down into three categories:

- **Technical controls**: The security controls (that is, safeguards or countermeasures) for an information system that are primarily implemented and executed by the information system through mechanisms contained in the hardware, software, or firmware components of the system
- **Management controls**: The security controls (that is, safeguards or countermeasures) for an information system that focuses on the management of risk and the management of information system security
- **Operational controls**: The security controls (that is, safeguards or countermeasures) for an information system that primarily are implemented and executed by people (as opposed to systems)

More information on information security policies is as follows:

Policy Area	Policy Families	Policy Topic Examples
Technical	Access Control Audit and Accountability Identification and Authentication System and Communications Protection	Account Management End User Device Security Server Security Controls Network Security Controls Web Based Application Controls
Management	Planning Risk Assessment Security Assessment Systems and Services Acquisitions	Information Security Program Establishment of Official Roles Information Security Metrics Conducting Risk Assessments Vulnerability Scanning Penetration Testing Account Rights Reviews
Operational	Awareness and Training Configuration Management Contingency Planning Incident Response Maintenance Media Protection Personnel Security Physical and Environmental Protection System and Information Integrity	Training Topics Expected and Prohibited Behavior Employee Screening Account Termination Business Continuity Planning Disaster Recovery Incident Response Planning Workplace Security Removable Device Security Sensitive Data Security

Planning policy

A planning policy in this context has to do with developing the information security program. This policy sets the foundation for an organization's information security program and is one of the initial activities that should be undertaken when an organization is beginning to mature its information security capability. Additionally, this policy establishes rules around the development, documentation, periodic update, and implementation of security plans for organizational information systems.

A planning policy should address:

- The establishment of organizational roles—CIO, CISO, system owner, data owner, data custodian, and so on
- What should be included and what should the update frequency be for the information security program plan?
- What artifacts should be developed to ensure repeatable processes around information security control selection, development, and implementation?

Access control policy

The purpose of access controls in an information system is to determine what activities are allowed and what activities are prohibited. Users, in most cases, should not have unfettered access to information systems. Access controls allow organizations to establish rules around how they want users to access information systems.

An access control policy should address:

- Limiting information system access to authorized users, processes acting on behalf of authorized users, or devices (including other information systems)
- Limiting information system access to the types of transactions and functions that authorized users are permitted to execute
- Controlling the flow of information in accordance with approved authorizations
- Separating the duties of individuals to reduce the risk of malevolent activity without collusion
- Employing the principle of least privilege, including for specific security functions and privileged accounts
- Using non-privileged accounts or roles when accessing non-security functions
- Preventing non-privileged users from executing privileged functions and auditing the execution of such functions
- Limiting unsuccessful logon attempts
- Providing privacy and security notices consistent with applicable rules
- Using session lock with pattern-hiding displays to prevent accessing/viewing of data after periods of inactivity
- Terminating (automatically) a user session after a defined condition

- Monitoring and controlling remote access sessions
- Employing cryptographic mechanisms to protect the confidentiality of remote access sessions
- Routing remote access via managed access control points
- Authorizing remote execution of privileged commands and remote access to security-relevant information
- Authorizing wireless access prior to allowing such connections
- Protecting wireless access using authentication and encryption
- Controlling the connection of mobile devices
- Encrypting information on mobile devices
- Verifying and controlling/limiting connections to and the use of external information systems
- Limiting the use of organizational portable storage devices on external information systems
- Controlling information posted or processed on publicly accessible information systems

Awareness and training policy

An awareness and training policy provides the foundation for organization-wide cybersecurity communications. The policy should address all levels of the organization from a management (CEO to line employee) and technical (systems, network, database administrator, and so on) perspective. The policy should also address the types of training that the organization will conduct, as well as its recurrence.

An awareness and training policy should address:

- Ensuring that managers and users of organizational information systems are made aware of the security risks associated with their activities and of the applicable laws, directives, policies, standards, instructions, regulations, or procedures related to the security of organizational information systems
- Ensuring that organizational personnel are adequately trained to carry out their assigned information security-related duties and responsibilities
- Providing security awareness training on recognizing and reporting potential indicators of an insider threat.

Auditing and accountability policy

Auditing and accountability policies establish the rules for how an information system securely alerts, records, stores, and allows access to auditable events important to information security. This policy also provides rules around audit log management that allow the high volume of audit logs that an information system produces to be manageable by the information security professional.

An auditing and accountability policy should address:

- Creating, protecting, and retaining information system audit records to the extent needed to enable the monitoring, analysis, investigation, and reporting of unlawful, unauthorized, or inappropriate information system activity
- Ensuring that the actions of individual information system users can be uniquely traced to those users so they can be held accountable for their actions
- Reviewing and updating audited events
- Alerting in the event of an audit process failure
- Correlating audit review, analysis, and reporting of processes for investigation and response to indications of inappropriate, suspicious, or unusual activity
- Providing audit reduction and report generation to support on-demand analysis and reporting
- Providing an information system capability that compares and synchronizes internal system clocks with an authoritative source to generate timestamps for audit records
- Protecting audit information and audit tools from unauthorized access, modification, and deletion
- Limiting management of audit functionality to a subset of privileged users

Configuration management policy

The configuration management policy establishes rules to ensure that changes to the information system are minimally disruptive to the functioning of the information system and the users that it supports. The configuration management policy also establishes rules that require IT professionals to document and track changes to an information system.

What the configuration management policy should address:

- Establishing and maintaining baseline configurations and inventories of organizational information systems (including hardware, software, firmware, and documentation) throughout the respective system development life cycles
- Establishing and enforcing security configuration settings for information technology products employed in organizational information systems
- Tracking, reviewing, approving/disapproving, and auditing changes to information systems
- Analyzing the security impact of changes prior to implementation
- Defining, documenting, approving, and enforcing physical and logical access restrictions associated with changes to the information system
- Employing the principle of least functionality by configuring the information system to provide only essential capabilities
- Restricting, disabling, and preventing the use of non-essential programs, functions, ports, protocols, and services
- Applying deny-by-exception (blacklisting) policies to prevent the use of unauthorized software or deny all, permit-by-exception (whitelisting) policies, to allow the execution of authorized software
- Controlling and monitoring user-installed software

Contingency planning policy

The contingency planning policy establishes the rules for an organization whereby it is able to effectively recover from an IT event that can range from a small service disruption to a catastrophic event where data processing capabilities have been rendered inaccessible.

What the contingency planning policy should address: the establishing, maintaining, and effectively implementing plans for emergency response, backup operations, and post-disaster recovery for organizational information systems to ensure the availability of critical information resources and continuity of operations in emergency situations.

Identification and authentication policy

The identification and authentication policy defines the organization's rules for information system identifiers that are provisioned and managed, as well as the mechanisms allowed for positive authentication of provisioned information system identifiers.

What the identification and authentication policy should address:

- Identifying information system users, processes acting on behalf of users, or devices
- Authenticating (or verifying) the identities of those users, processes, or devices as a prerequisite to allowing access to organizational information systems
- Using multifactor authentication for local and network access to information systems
- Employing replay-resistant authentication mechanisms for network access to privileged and non-privileged accounts
- Preventing reuse of identifiers for a defined period
- Disabling identifiers after a defined period of inactivity
- Enforcing a minimum password complexity and change of characters when new passwords are created
- Prohibiting password reuse for a specified number of generations
- Allowing temporary password use for system logons with an immediate change to a permanent password
- Storing and transmitting only encrypted representation of passwords
- Obscuring feedback of authentication information

Incident response policy

The incident response policy is responsible for identifying the required actions necessary related to reporting, responding, and incident handling related to information security incidents.

What the incident response policy should address:

- Establishing an operational incident handling capability for organizational information systems that includes adequate preparation, detection, analysis, containment, recovery, and user response activities
- Tracking, documenting, and reporting incidents to appropriate organizational officials and/or authorities
- Testing the organizational incident response capability

Maintenance policy

The maintenance policy establishes rules for how an information system should be managed specific to information security. There will be additional policies maintained by an IT organization around operations and maintenance.

What the maintenance policy should address:

- Performing periodic and timely maintenance on organizational information systems
- Providing effective controls on the tools, techniques, mechanisms, and personnel used to conduct information system maintenance
- Ensuring equipment removed for off-site maintenance is sanitized of any information
- Checking media containing diagnostic and test programs for malicious code before the media is used in the information system
- Requiring multifactor authentication to establish nonlocal maintenance sessions via external network connections and terminate such connections when nonlocal maintenance is complete
- Supervising the maintenance activities of maintenance personnel without required access authorization

Media protection policy

The media protection policy is responsible for defining how media will be handled within the organization. This includes secure handling, what media is allowed, how media should be protected, and how media should be destroyed.

What the media protection policy should address:

- Protecting information system media, both paper and digital
- Limiting access to information on information system media to authorized users
- Sanitizing or destroying information system media before disposal or release for reuse
- Marking media with necessary markings and distribution limitations
- Controlling access to media and maintaining accountability for media during transport outside of controlled areas

- Implementing cryptographic mechanisms to protect the confidentiality of information stored on digital media during transport, unless otherwise protected by alternative physical safeguards
- Controlling the use of removable media on information system components
- Prohibiting the use of portable storage devices when such devices have no identifiable owner
- Protecting the confidentiality of backup information at storage locations

Personnel security policy

The personnel security policy establishes rules that have to do with ensuring that organizational team members can be trusted to perform sensitive IT work.

What the personnel security policy should address:

- Ensuring that individuals occupying positions of responsibility within organizations (including third-party service providers) are trustworthy and meet established security criteria for those positions
- Ensuring that organizational information and information systems are protected during and after personnel actions such as terminations and transfers
- Employing formal sanctions for personnel failing to comply with organizational security policies and procedures

Physical and environmental protection policy

The physical and environmental policy establishes rules that ensure that the building where sensitive data processing occurs is secure from a personnel perspective as well as from a physical plant perspective.

What the physical and environmental policy should address:

- Limiting physical access to information systems, equipment, and the respective operating environments to authorized individuals
- Protecting the physical plant and support infrastructure for information systems
- The development of supporting utilities for information systems
- Protecting information systems against environmental hazards

- Providing appropriate environmental controls in facilities containing information systems
- Escorting visitors and monitoring visitor activity
- Maintaining audit logs of physical access
- Controlling and managing physical access devices
- Enforcing safeguarding measures for information at alternate work sites (for example, telework sites)

Risk assessment policy

The risk assessment policy establishes the rules for the organization that explains how the organization will conduct risk assessments at the organizational, operational, and system-specific level.

What the risk assessment policy should address:

- Assessing risk to organizational operations (including mission, functions, image, or reputation), organizational assets, and individuals, resulting from the operation of organizational information systems and the associated processing, storage, or transmission of organizational information
- Scanning for vulnerabilities in the information system and applications periodically and when new vulnerabilities affecting the system are identified
- Remediating vulnerabilities in accordance with assessments of risk

Security assessment policy

The security assessment policy establishes rules for how the organization will conduct information security testing on a new information system or information system components. This policy also establishes the rules for how information security continuous monitoring and reporting will be established for the organization.

What the security assessment policy should address:

- The periodic assessment of security controls in organizational information systems to determine if the controls are effective in their application
- The development and implementation of plans of action designed to correct deficiencies and reduce or eliminate vulnerabilities in organizational information systems

- The authorization to operational and organizational information systems and any associated information system connections by management
- The monitoring of information system security controls on an ongoing basis to ensure the continued effectiveness of the controls

System and communications protection policy

The systems and communications protection policy establishes the rules necessary to properly establish network segmentation and boundary protection thought the organization, as well as establishing the necessary rules around how cryptography will be implemented. Additionally, this policy establishes rules around allowed communication methods and mechanisms to ensure that the authenticity of those methods is maintained.

What the system and communications policy should address:

- Monitoring, controlling, and protecting organizational communications (that is, information transmitted or received by organizational information systems) at the external boundaries and key internal boundaries of the information systems
- Employing architectural designs, software development techniques, and systems engineering principles that promote effective information security within organizational information systems
- Implementing subnetworks for publicly accessible system components that are physically or logically separated from internal networks
- Denying network communications traffic by default and allowing network communications traffic by exception (that is, deny all, permit by exception)
- Preventing remote devices from simultaneously establishing non-remote connections with the information system and communicating via some other connection to resources in external networks
- Implementing cryptographic mechanisms to prevent unauthorized disclosure of information during transmission unless otherwise protected by alternative physical safeguards
- Terminating network connections associated with communication sessions at the end of the sessions or after a defined period of inactivity
- Establishing and managing cryptographic keys for cryptography employed in the information system
- Employing cryptography to protect the confidentiality of system information
- Prohibiting remote activation of collaborative computing devices and provide an indication of devices in use to users present at the device

- Controlling and monitoring the use of mobile codes
- Controlling and monitoring the use of **Voice over Internet Protocol** (**VoIP**) technologies
- Protecting the authenticity of communication sessions
- Protecting the confidentiality of information at rest

System and information integrity policy

The system and information integrity protection policy establishes rules around information system monitoring, updating, patching, scanning, and remediating. The purpose of these activities is to ensure that information system-critical IT hygiene components are functioning and well maintained.

What the system and information integrity policy should address:

- Identifying, reporting, and correcting information and information system flaws in a timely manner
- Providing protection from malicious code at appropriate locations within organizational information systems
- Monitoring information system security alerts and advisories and taking appropriate actions in response
- Updating malicious code protection mechanisms when new releases are available
- Performing periodic scans of the information system and real-time scans of files from external sources as files are downloaded, opened, or executed
- Monitoring the information system including inbound and outbound communications traffic, to detect attacks and indicators of potential attacks
- Identifying unauthorized use of the information system

Systems and services acquisitions policy

The purpose of the systems and services acquisition policy is to ensure that the information security program is properly inserted into the acquisitions life cycle of an organization, helping to ensure that secure and safe products are procured for the organization. Additionally, this policy ties-in the need for an effective SDLC approach, with information security being a key player.

What the system and services acquisitions policy should address:

- Allocating sufficient resources to adequately protect organizational information systems
- Employing system development life cycle processes that incorporate information security considerations
- Employing software usage and installation restrictions
- Ensuring that third-party providers employ adequate security measures to protect information, applications, and/or services outsourced from the organization

Summary

In this chapter, we discussed the critical activities required to establish an enterprise-wide information security program, focusing on executive buy-in, policies, procedures, standards, and guidelines.

In this chapter, you learned:

- The planning concept related to information security program establishment
- Success factors for information security program success
- Information security program integration into organizational processes
- Maturity concepts related to information security program planning
- Policies, procedures, standards, and guidelines

In the next chapter, we will be covering the concepts of information security risk management. We will be discussing who has the responsibility for risk ownership within the organization and how to perform a risk assessment.

4

Information Security Risk Management

In this chapter, we will be discussing information security risk management, which provides the main interface between the information security program and the business for prioritization and communication.

In this chapter, you will learn:

- Key information security risk management concepts
- Determining where valuable data is located
- Quick risk assessment techniques
- How risk management affects different parts of the organization
- How to perform information categorization
- Security control selection, implementation, and testing
- Authorizing information systems for production operations

What is risk?

Information security risk comes into play when there is a potential event or circumstance that could lead to organizational disruption, damage to organizational reputation, or financial loss because of failure of an information system.

The goal of information security risk management is to minimize the overall risk to an organization, as well as people, processes, and technology related to the information systems within an organization.

Risk management involves the entire organization, from senior executives down to front-line employees. This highly complex process requires a thorough understanding of how people, processes, and technology interact in the organization at all levels.

Who owns organizational risk?

Risk ownership is a very important topic and is given careful attention today in light of large-scale breaches in government and private sector information systems. In the past, many organizations viewed information security risk as being something that was the responsibility of the IT division of an organization. While this is not, and has never been, an acceptable practice it is how many organizations effectively viewed the ownership of risk within their organization.

The issue that many organizations encounter is the concept of risk ownership versus risk management.

Risk ownership

Understanding risk ownership, and who does not own risk, is critically important in order to make the correct risk decisions that support your organization's business and mission objectives:

- Risk ownership is held by the C-suite and/or people at the boardroom level.
- The ability to own risk is tied to authority and the ability to commit funds to reduce risk.
- Senior leaders have the ability to fund risk reduction efforts as well as the ability to change the direction of organizational efforts and culture.
- It is critically important that risks to the organization be effectively communicated to senior leadership with effective, well thought out plans to reduce risk.
- While risk ownership sits with the executive team of an organization, it is the responsibility of the information security professional to deliver the facts regarding organizational risk coupled with the necessary plans of action to reduce the risk to acceptable levels.
- This is where an effective understanding of the organization comes into play. Senior leadership will not be receptive to your risk reduction strategies if they do not align with the organizational mission.

What is risk management?

Risk management and risk ownership are two very different things. While risk ownership is an executive/board responsibility, risk management is a delegated responsibility that extends throughout the organization:

- While risk ownership sits with the most senior leaders of an organization, risk management is a team sport.
- Risk management spans from the most junior front-line employee up to senior management.
- Risk management duties are delegated down from the senior management.
- Risk acceptance cannot be delegated. Risk acceptance decisions must be made by the risk owners and must be communicated effectively by the risk managers.

 It is a very common trap for an IT professional to fall into to think that they are the risk owner because they are responsible for an information system. The IT professional may be inclined to make decisions that relate to the risk of an IT system that they are not authorized to make, which can lead to an inadvertent exposure for the organization. Risk should be communicated up the organizational hierarchy to the risk owners via a repeatable risk management process.

Where is your valuable data?

Understanding your organization's valuable data is a key component of a successful information security program. Without an adequate understanding of your organization's critical business information you, as the information security professional, will be unable to adequately ensure that your organization's interests are adequately protected.

The information security program must align with key business stakeholders to help understand what the most valuable pieces of information are in the organization so that you can work with the business and IT teams to secure the data.

What does my organization have that is worth protecting?

Information security is not about implementing new information security tools. It is about protecting your organization's sensitive information assets. As an information security professional, you must determine what is important to your organization so that you can prioritize your security activities.

Intellectual property trade secrets

- Does your organization have intellectual property or trade secrets?
- Does your organization have competitors that would benefit from having access to this information?
- Does your organization maintain intellectual property or trade secrets on digital systems?

Personally Identifiable Information – PII

- Does your organization collect personally identifiable information for your employees, customers, or partners?
    - Standard PII is information that can often be gathered from the telephone book and includes names, birthdates, or addresses
- Does your organization collect sensitive PII?
    - Sensitive PII is information that is not readily available to the public and includes social security numbers, tax ID numbers, and unlisted telephone numbers

Personal Health Information – PHI

- Does your organization collect personal health information for your employees, customers, or partners?
- PHI includes medical history, demographic information, insurance information, laboratory and test results, and any other data that a healthcare provider collects to establish identity and determine care.

General questions

Does the organization have any information that, if exposed, would cause our customers to lose confidence in the organization? For example:

- **Retail**: Loss of payment card data
- **Government**: Loss of PII information

Does your organization have any information that, if exposed, could potentially severely impact revenue? For example:

- **Government contractor**: Loss of government customer information
- **Food processor**: Loss of proprietary formulas

Questions for the business manager:

- Is there information that, if lost, would cause you to lose your job?
- Is there any information that your business unit requires to function? Without this information your business unit will stop functioning.
- Is there any specific information that keeps you awake at night?

Performing a quick risk assessment

The purpose of the quick risk assessment in this book is to give you a pulse check for your organization. The purpose is not to replace the more detailed risk assessment procedures detailed in this chapter. Use this quick assessment to give yourself and management a down-and-dirty review of what your organization, business partners, or vendors look like from an information security perspective. When presenting the output of this quick assessment you should ensure that you let your management know that this is a pulse check, and that they should expect more to come from an information security risk perspective.

Instructions:

- **Yes**: 5 points
- **Unsure**: 5 points
- **No**: 0 points

Answer the following questions with the preceding numerical scores. Once completed, add up your answers to determine your score. Compare your score to the following range to determine your risk rating:

- Does your organization use an internal unsecured guest wireless network?
- Does your organization allow the use of personal devices on the organizational network?
- Does your organization allow high-risk information systems connected to the internet?
- Does your organization have the ability to securely dispose of sensitive hardcopy media and are your employees trained on how to dispose of the media?
- Does your organization allow regular users (non-IT users) privileged (administrative) access to any network device or computer?
- Does your organization allow the use of unrestricted **Universal Serial Bus** (**USB**) connections?
- Do employees or customers access internal information systems from remote locations with a VPN?
- Does your organization have information security policies and are they fully enforced?
- Does your organization use cloud-based software or storage?
- Does your organization allow the use of personal devices for business use or on a company network?
- Does your organization use information systems to store personally identifiable information of customers or employees?
- Does your organization have third-party suppliers, vendors, or partners that are network interconnected?
- Does your organization conduct business with foreign countries?
- Does your organization have an acceptable use policy and do you fully enforce the policy?
- Does your organization install anti-malware software and is that software properly configured, updated, and monitored?
- Does your organization have a password expiration policy and is that policy fully enforced?
- Does your organization conduct information security awareness training for every user that that has access to organizational information systems?
- Does your organization store sensitive information that could potentially compromise its ability to continue business if ex-filtrated (intellectual property, government information, financial records, payment card data, and so on)?

- Does your organization control access into and out of your building utilizing a mechanism to positively ID everyone?
- Has your organization implemented and tested disaster recovery capabilities for critical systems?

Quick risk assessment scoring:

- Critical risk: 55-100
- High risk: 30-50
- Moderate risk: 15-25
- Low risk: 0-10

Risk management is an organization-wide activity

Managing information security risk is a highly complex activity that requires the information security professional to be actively involved in all facets of the organization, from top-level organizational leadership down to the people, processes, and technology that makes the organization's mission successful:

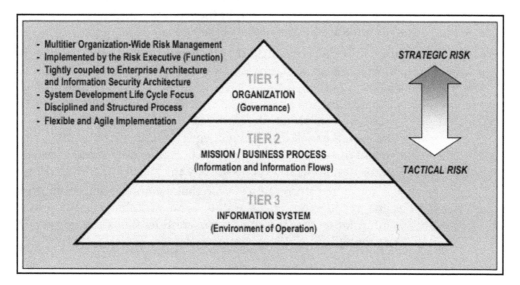

The information professional must establish a risk management strategy whereby an organization can establish repeatable mechanisms for the ongoing assessment, response, and monitoring of information security risks. This allows the information security professional to engage the organization in a repeatable and transparent way, helping to ensure a greater level of acceptance by the organization. Use the following examples as a guide as you begin the process of understanding your organization more deeply.

Business operations

Business operations staff focus on the successful operations of the organization and are typically business/mission focused:

- Examples include: Finance, HR, and manufacturing.
- Looking at business operations is a key activity for properly understanding the following.
- What level of risk will a business unit be willing to accept as it relates to an information system:
    - An e-commerce business unit may be willing to accept a higher level of risk for an internal collaboration server versus its e-commerce website
    - A manufacturing business unit may place a high value on an internal collaboration server that contains highly sensitive proprietary information
- You must work with a given business unit to understand the criticality of the data that an information system is processing. Not all data needs to be protected at the same level:
    - An information system may contain publicly available and accessible information. While this information needs to be protected to ensure that its integrity and availability are maintained, the confidentiality concern is deemed low since the information must be accessible by the public.
    - A different information system that contains intellectual property may result in a high-risk rating because of the need to protect the information that it contains, and confidentiality, integrity, and availability.

IT operations

- How is your enterprise's information technology architected?
    - For example, for a web-based application that is accessible to internal employees, you should ask questions such as the following:
        - Does the application need to be accessible from the internet so that remote employees can access it?
        - If external remote access to the organization is required can a VPN be used?
        - Is multi-factor authentication available to secure the users' authenticator?

Personnel

- How does your organization onboard new staff members?
    - Do repeatable processes exist to ensure that new staff members get the correct permissions and have access to only the information and information systems that they need to do their jobs?
    - Do processes exist to onboard contractors and partners in a similar fashion as mentioned previously for staff members?

 A very common issue that an organization will often experience is building solid repeatable processes for their internal staff members, and only having ad hoc processes in place for contractors and partners. Ensure that you build a process that includes everyone that will require access to your organization's data and information systems.

- How does your organization out-process staff members?
    - As previously mentioned, ensure that any process includes internal staff, contractors, and partners.
    - Does your organization have a mechanism where HR informs IT that staff members are leaving so that rights can be revoked?
    - How are application owners notified of changes in employment? IT may be notified and network access may be revoked, however application access may still be enabled

After an employee, contractor, or partner leaves a company, application access is often still in place. It is very important that a process exists to notify everyone that has IT administration capabilities in an organization. It is important to remember that not all IT administration exists under the **chief information officer**. In most cases, the user administration of business applications is performed by business units (finance manages the accounting system, HR manages the HRIS system, and so on). The points of contact for these systems must be notified when someone has left the service of an organization.

- How do you monitor personnel?
  - Do you have policies and training in place that clearly sets expectations regarding privacy and monitoring of users?
  - What technological capabilities do you have in place?
    - Do you have a DLP solution that can ensure that users are unable to send sensitive corporate data to unauthorized users or networks?
    - Have you deployed a solution such as information rights management in Office 365 (`https://technet.microsoft.com/en-us/library/dn792011.aspx`) that allows you to revoke access to information regardless of its location?
    - Do you have a **Cloud Access Security Broker (CASB)**, which allows you to define rules for a user's access to information in a cloud environment?

External organization

Vendors:

- Do you inspect the tools that are brought into your enterprise to manage information systems as part of a contract?
  - Contract SLAs will not prevent your organization from receiving malware from infected vendor devices
- Do you monitor third-party connections from vendors?
  - These connections can serve as a conduit for data exfiltration or malware infections

Subcontractors/partners:

- Are your subcontractors required to follow the same information security requirements as you?
  - This can pose a serious concern to any contracts that you may have where compliance is a key performance requirement
- Do subcontractors use their own equipment or yours in commissions of contract activities?

Subsidiaries/divisions:

- Is your information technology organization centralized or decentralized?
  - Does corporate IT policy exist that applies to all of the organization?
  - Do mechanisms exist to ensure that corporate policy is adhered to and are there consequences?
    - Will an information system be disconnected from the network, or will it be given a reasonable amount of time depending on the infraction to remedy the situation?

Looking at factors such as these are part of the risk management process and allows an information security professional to gain a holistic understanding of how the organization operates as it relates to people, processes, and technology from both a business and IT perspective. This better informs the information security professional as it relates to the risk of a new IT component being introduced to the organization.

Risk management life cycle

Risk management is key to the successful implementation of an organizational information security program. The risk management framework as defined in, *SP 800-37 Rev. 1*, NIST Special Publication 800-37 Revision 1 established a detailed life cycle for the identification and management of risk for information and information systems:

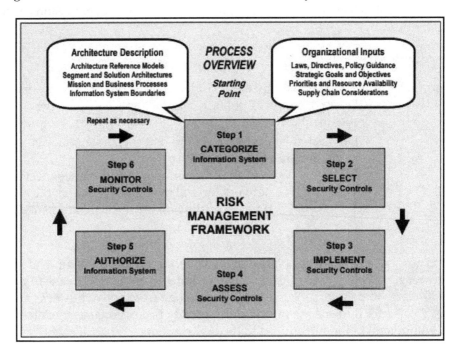

Information categorization

The information security professional must work with the organization's business and IT groups to properly classify the data used by the organization to successfully complete its mission. Data classification is a key initial step in establishing a strong information security program. The process of conducting data classification exercises with business leaders within your organization will allow the organization's leader to be part of the decision-making process for how data will be secured within the organization and how resources will be applied. By conducting this process, you, as the information security professional, ensure that you are highlighting the critical information assets of the organization and are applying information security controls where needed, to support your organization's mission.

We will spend more time on this part of the risk management life cycle than any other subject in this book. The process of information categorization is a foundational point, where you are working with your business leaders and are able to develop requirements that can be used to secure the future information technology environment. While certainly not being a technically glitzy phase it is truly one of the most important phases of the risk management life cycle.

Data classification looks to understand

- What information assets are within your organization?
- What is the value of those assets to your organization?
- What will it take to properly secure those assets commensurate with their value?

An organization's information systems are jam-packed with data that is required for the organization to accomplish its mission. It is important when you begin the process of performing data categorization that you understand that not all data is made equal, and therefore, not all data has the same value to the organization. As a result, you will not be applying the same security controls to protect all data throughout the organization as this would result in wasting resources.

If you reserve your most difficult-to-implement and most costly security controls for data that has the highest value to the organization you will be establishing an efficient and cost-conscious information protection program. This is a key component to a successful information security program as it establishes the following:

- **Trust in the information security program**: Your information security program should be able to distinguish between sensitive and non-sensitive information. Additionally, it should be able to provide tailored guidance regarding how to protect the different types of information. Not doing this will cause the organization to do unnecessary work for some subset of your corporate data, causing frustration with project and finance teams.

- **Fiscal responsibility**: A key part of a successful information security program is senior leadership support. One way to ensure that you lose your leadership's support is to waste their resources. By selecting only the needed security controls for a particular type of organizational data, you are showing your leadership that you are committed to saving the organization money and that you value the resources that you have been given.

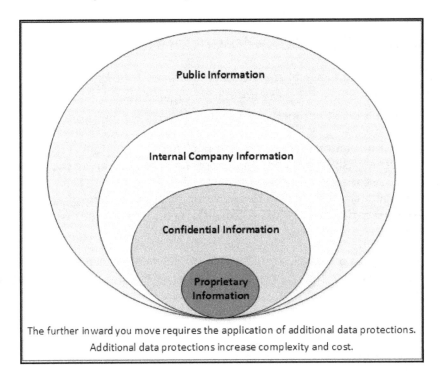

As an information security professional conducting data classification you must ensure that you properly identify organizational data, properly apply the most prudent security controls, and ensure that the organization's resources are being maximized and used efficiently.

Data classification steps

There are four steps associated with data classification:

1. Determine organizational information assets
2. Find organizational information within the information system

3. Organize data into protection categories
4. Assign a value to your information

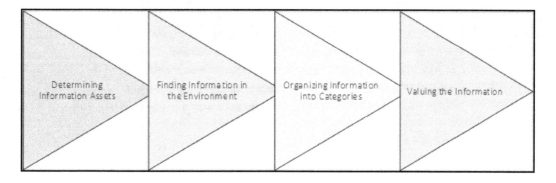

Determining information assets

Determining what the organization's information assets are can be a pretty complicated activity. Often, when an organization wants to understand their information they go to IT looking for the answer. However, in this case, we need to work with the organization's business groups. The information technology group typically does not know the context behind the data they are storing. They are worried about storage volume size and read/write speed. It is the business units that can provide context behind what the data actually means and why it is important to their business function.

Sample questions to ask when determining your organization's information assets:

- Does your organization process transactional information such as orders, payments, and/or invoices?
- Does the organization have sensitive sales and marketing information related to its products and services?
- Does the organization have specific product offerings and does the organization have information related to its product development?
- Does your organization store information related to its customers, suppliers, and/or partners?

The information you should gather:

Information Type	Information Purpose	Information Owner
Provide a clear descriptive title for the information.	Provide a business description for the information. This description would typically be provided by the information owner.	Provide the name of the individual in management that is ultimately responsible for this information. This is not typically a person in IT.
Examples		
Design Specifications	Specification for the new trans galactic star destroyer.	Suzie Sunshine
Product Pricing Information	The cost to develop the medium-sized space laser versus the actual selling price.	John Doe

Finding information in the environment

Now that we have identified the information types within our organization we need to understand where this information resides within the information system. You may find that your business users might not be able to help as much now that we are starting to look for the information within the IT environment. However, your business users should be able to point you in the right direction. Ask them who they work with in the IT organization when using their services. Ask them how they access their information and what the path is to that location. From a business user perspective, you may quickly find this is all they can give you. On a positive note, your business users should be able to provide this level of detail. This information is a great start, then you can go back to the IT team and start tracking down where the business information resides.

Now that you have some basic information from your business users you can take this to your IT department and begin hunting down the physical location of the data. You may need to work with various members of your IT department, including the following:

- Information and system architects
- Database administrators
- System administrators
- Network administrators

More than likely, the data that you discover based on your interviews with business users does not exist on a single server. Modern information systems have components that are spread across multiple physical servers.

For example, in the case of a web-based application a properly architected application will sit across three tiers:

1. **Presentation tier**: This is the top-most level of the application stack and comprises the user interface.
2. **Logic tier**: This level of the application stack communicates between the presentation and data tier. This part of the stack performs calculations, processes commands, makes decisions, and so on.
3. **Data tier**: This is the lowest level of the application stack. This part of the stack stores that data of the application.

 Note: Each of these tiers could contain multiple servers for redundancy.

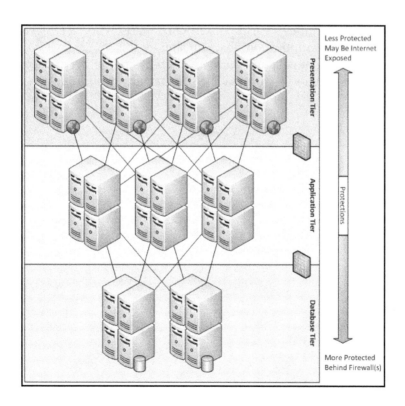

In the preceding example, you can see that a simple URL provided by a business user could easily expand out into 36 servers with 12 application interconnections across 3 security zones. This is information that the average business user would not have and that the IT team will have readily available.

While the information storage exists within the database tier, the totality of the application must be considered when it comes to information as the data is processed and manipulated by the entire application.

Disaster recovery considerations

Disaster recovery architecture must be taken into account as you review the information location for sensitive business data. The same level of security must be applied for all parts of the information system to properly protect business information based on the business requirements.

- In the following example, the inclusion of a disaster recovery site has doubled the number of server and applications from the previous example to 64 servers and 24 application interconnections
- This example includes a backup internet connection and a representation of data replication at the application's backup site:
    - If not properly secured, the backup internet connection could be used as a pathway into the backup application

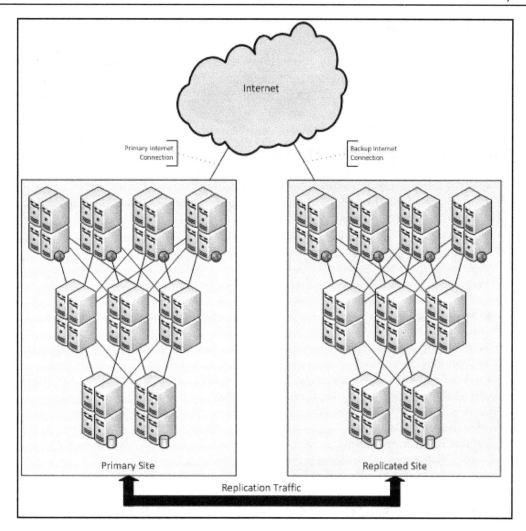

Backup storage considerations

Backup storage must be considered as you are working to identify the location of business data with the organization's information system:

- The backup storage environment must be protected at the same level as the business information requirement.
- It is important to ensure that backup media is secured at all times from unauthorized access.

- Unnecessary backup copies should be destroyed in accordance with your organization's policies:
    - Unnecessary copies of an information system backup could become mismanaged over time leading to unauthorized access. If you don't need it anymore get rid of it!

Types of storage options

- **Virtual machine snapshot**: This type of backup makes a point in time copy of a virtual machine disk file. This can be used to restore a virtual machine to a particular point in time.
- **Disk backup**: Because the storage is not linear, such as tape, individual files can be directly accessed allowing for faster recovery times.

    It provides a higher capacity and speed than tape.

- **Tape backup**: Liner storage mechanism used for long-term archival storage.

    Going out of favor due to the lowering in costs associated with disk-based backup

- **Cloud backup**: This utilizing a service like Amazon Web Services to provide backup services versus an internal backup mechanism.

    The information security professional must make take care when reviewing the cloud backup provider contract ensuring that the backup provider meets all of the information security requirements for the business' information.

Questions you should ask your business users regarding their information's location

- Does the business user have an IT point of contact for the information system that contains their data (managerial, administrative, and/or helpdesk)?
- Does the business user use a Windows file share to store or process their information?
- Does the business user use a web application to store or process their information?

Questions you should ask your IT organization regarding the information's location

- Is the information shared with multiple information systems?
    - For example, a financial system will typically provide data to human resources and external business partners
- Is the information synced or replicated across multiple servers?
- How is the information backed up?

Information Type	Information Purpose	Information Location	Information Owner
Provide a clear descriptive title for the information.	Provide a business description for the information. This description would typically be provided by the information owner.	Provide the specific location where the information resides on the information system.	Provide the name of the individual in management that is ultimately responsible for this information. This is not typically a person in IT.
		Examples	
Design Specifications	Specification for the new trans galactic star destroyer.	**Application Name:** Windows File Share **IP Address :** 10.53.11.6 **Server Name:** SenFS **Server UNC Path:** \\SenFS\Designs\Destroyer	Suzie Sunshine
Product Pricing Information	The cost to develop the medium-sized space laser versus the actual selling price.	**Application Name:** Product Pricing Application **IP Address :** 10.53.11.1 **Server Name:** ProdP **Application URL:** https://prodp.org.local/product_pricing	John Doe

Organizing information into categories

Now that you have determined what your organization's information assets are and where they are located within your organization's information system you can now begin the process of further categorizing the information.

The purpose behind this step is to place the information that you have identified into categories that will help the business and IT organization build information security controls for the protection of this information.

Examples of information type categories

The following are some examples of information category types and how to think about them from a confidentiality, integrity, and availability perspective:

Publicly available information

- Includes information that you would generally include on your web page or social media
- The CIA triad:
    - **Confidentiality**: Would typically be low as the general public would need to access it without authentication
    - **Integrity**: Would be moderate or high based on your organization's policies, as you would not want the information on your public web page replaced by an attacker
    - **Availability**: Would depend on organizational policy:
        - An e-commerce site would be high for availability
        - A blog may be designated as low or moderate dependent on the criticality to the organization

Credit card information

- Includes information related to a credit card. This information can be printed on the card, stored within the card, or processed and transmitted as part of an electronic transaction.

- The CIA triad:
  - **Confidentiality**: Would be at least moderate and could be high depending on your organizational policies, as credit card information must be protected from unauthorized use
  - **Integrity**: Would be at least moderate or high based on your organization's policies
  - **Availability**: Would be at least moderate or high based on your organization's policies

Trade secrets

The *Uniform Trade Secrets Act* defines a trade secret as follows:

- Information, including a formula, pattern, compilation, program, device, method, technique, or process
- It derives independent economic value, actual or potential, from not being generally known to or readily ascertainable through appropriate means by other persons who might obtain economic value from its disclosure or use; and
- Is the subject of efforts that are reasonable under the circumstances to maintain its secrecy.
- The CIA triad:
  - Confidentiality, integrity, and availability would all be, at minimum, moderate. However, it is likely that CIA would be placed into the high category for this data type due to the business criticality of the data.

When creating information categories, the goal is not to create too many. The more categories that you create, the more difficult it will be to manage your information security architecture in the future.

Take the information category of publicly available information mentioned previously. In this example, both the organization's public website and the data posted to social media can placed into this category. You would not want to create a separate category for the public website and social media as this would be an unending cycle of category creation.

By using a single category such as publicly available information to capture the information type, we can potentially place hundreds of pieces of information into a similar category, and which all require similar levels of protection:

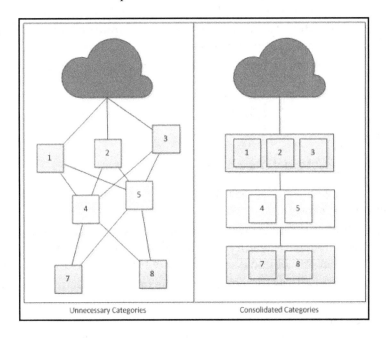

Unnecessary Categories | Consolidated Categories

From an operational perspective, some IT systems may have unique requirements. Still, by using the example of publicly available information as we translate this category into an architecture, we will be defining the rules for how the publicly available data network segment speaks to network segments at higher security levels, as well as the untrusted internet. The publicly available network segment will provide the basis for network security for the data and IT systems contained within it. However, each individual IT system will still have its own set of requirements related to allowable ports and protocols, application interconnections, and so on.

As you can see in the following example, an information category that translates into a network architecture still has additional requirements that relate to the applications that reside within the architecture. In this example, you have the information categories of publicly accessible data and internal company data expressed in real-word information technology implementations. Equipment has been deployed and configuration has been established, which allow for the protection of information as established through careful analysis of business requirements.

Remember that you build information systems based on business requirements and not the better judgment of IT. If you are not working with your business stakeholders and developing information systems that meet their requirements you are not doing your job as an IT professional.

The following example also shows that their specific application configurations go beyond the configurations present within the network segments established through information categorization. These additional requirements ensure that the application has the necessary resources to communicate with end users and backend processes.

A key consideration when building an application within a segmented network environment is to not violate the segmentation rules in favor of convenience or poor planning. Remember that if organizational leaders have been consulted to establish these network segmentation rules they exist at the request of management. When building an application in a secured environment ensure that you include the environment's information security requirements so that you can properly plan for these requirements in the application design.

This also brings us back to an important point mentioned earlier in the book. Including the information security professional in the initiation phase of the design process per your organization's system design life cycle process will help to ensure that the proper security requirements are part of the overall application functional requirements. Doing this will help to ensure that convenience and poor planning decisions during the application design process are minimized or eliminated.

You should, however, improve the security of an application that resides in a segmented network. While designing your application, you should be considering how the application interconnects with its various components and how the user will access the application. The principle of least privilege should be used as part of the design, working to ensure that the application components expose the least amount of functionality to fully satisfy the business user's requirements.

Examples to consider:

- How will the user access the application?
  - Is this an internal-use-only application?
  - It may not require internet access.
  - Does the application require remote access?
  - Can the application be accessed via VPN?
  - Can a cloud-based application proxy be employed?

- How will the application components be interconnected?
    - Does the application require access to other applications in order to function? What are that application's information security requirements?
    - What is the minimum number of ports, protocols, and services required in order to get the application functioning?

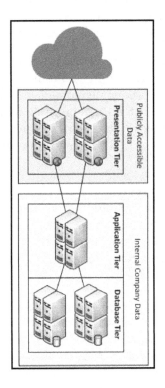

The following example shows how taking the information assets defined earlier can then be grouped into a fewer number of segments. As mentioned earlier, doing this allows you to simplify your network segmentation deployment and it makes it easier for the business to develop requirements around how they want to have their data protected.

There are no rules for how many information assets can sit within a specific information category so long as you can manage the category effectively. It is simply important to ensure that the assets within a single category have the same importance to the organization, and that they require the same level of protection. In the following example, we can clearly see that different types of data are located within the same categories.

In this example, the organization decided to use a simple approach to establishing categories so that they could effectively manage their environment. As you move from public information to proprietary information, you have an ever-increasing concern for the part of the organization as it relates to information protection, and an ever-increasing level of security at the network level from the information technology organization:

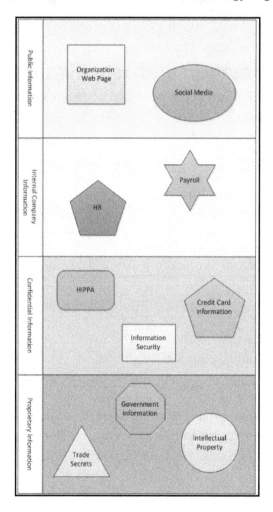

Two key points to remember about information categorization:

- Do not have too many information categories:
    - Too many categories will result in the following:
        1. Confusion on the part of organizational leaders
        2. An increase in information technology spending

- Don't force a needlessly small number of information categories:
  - If you need more, create more
  - Only create them when you absolutely need them
  - Creating too few could result in an increase in IT spending as information systems could have needless security controls applied to them

Valuing the information and establishing impact

In order to properly protect information, you must understand what the value of the information is to the organization and what impact it will cause if the information is stolen, lost, or destroyed.

Valuing information

Assigning value to the information that has been analyzed is a key final step to building the information security protection needed for your organization. Assigning a value to your organization's information will allow you to best decide how much money the organization should commit to protecting that information.

Example questions for assigning value to information are as follows:

- Consider the regulatory and compliance requirements for a certain information asset:
  - Are there specific fines?
  - Could a contract be lost?
- Consider what would happen to your organization if the data was to be lost, stolen, or modified:
  - What did it cost to develop the information or capability?
  - What is the impact of having another competitor?

Establishing impact

An important part of establishing the information value is assigning a qualitative score to the information that signifies the impact of lost, stolen, or destroyed information. By utilizing this score, you can establish appropriate security controls in order to properly protect your organizational information.

By utilizing the potential impact definitions from *NIST Special Publication 199* as a guide we will take the information that we gathered throughout the information categorization process to assign an impact rating to the information:

		Impact		
		Low	Moderate	High
CIA	**Confidentiality** has to do with whether information is kept secret or private. Mechanisms should be employed such as encryption, which would render the data useless if it was accessed in an unauthorized manner.	Unintended disclosure results in **limited** negative impact to the organization	Unintended disclosure results in **serious** negative impact to the organization	Unintended disclosure results in **catastrophic or severe** negative impact to the organization
	Integrity has to do with whether information is kept accurate. Information should not be modified in an unauthorized manner and safeguards should be in place that allow for detectable and timely unauthorized changes.	Unintended destruction or modification results in **limited** negative impact to the organization	Unintended destruction or modification results in **serious** negative impact to the organization	Unintended destruction or modification results in **catastrophic or severe** negative impact to the organization
	Availability has to do with ensuring that information is available when it is needed. This control can be accomplished by implementing tools ranging from battery backup at the data center to a Content Distribution Network in the cloud.	Access disruption results in a **limited** negative impact to the organization	Access disruption results in a **serious** negative impact to the organization	Access disruption results in a **catastrophic or severe** negative impact to the organization

We will use the design specification information type from the earlier example to show how to apply impact levels to our information. In the following example based on careful analysis by business, IT, and security stakeholders, the following impact levels have been assigned to the CIA triad. A watermark of *High* is used to define the overall impact for the information type and will be used to establish the future security control baseline:

Information type	Confidentiality	Integrity	Availability	High watermark
Design Specifications	High	Moderate	Moderate	High

Selecting the correct impact level is important from an information protection and financial perspective. Selecting too low of an impact value will result in inappropriately protected systems as well as more resources being applied to a system than is required, based on the data being protected.

Information Type	Information Purpose	Information Location	Information Owner	Information Risk If Disclosed	Information Value if Disclosed	Impact High Watermark
Provide a clear descriptive title for the information.	Provide the business description for the information. This description would typically be provided by the information owner.	Provide the specific location where the information resides on the information system.	Provide the name of the individual in management that is ultimately responsible for this information. This is not typically a person in IT.	Provide a brief description regarding the business risk of information disclosure	Provide the estimated value the business assigns to the information.	Provide the high water mark value defined as part of establishing the information impact if lost

Example						
Design Specifications	Specification for the new trans galactic star destroyer.	**Application Name:** Windows File Share **IP Address :** 10.53.11.6 **Server Name:** SenFS **Server UNC Path:** \\SenFS\Designs\Destroyer	Suzie Sunshine	If this information is disclosed potential competitors will be able to build their own star destroyers.	$100 Billion	High
Product Pricing Information	The cost to develop the medium-sized space laser versus the actual selling price.	**Application Name:** Product Pricing Application **IP Address :** 10.53.11.1 **Server Name:** ProdP **Application URL:** https://prodp.org.local/product_pricing	John Doe	If this information is disclosed competitors will understand our pricing strategy allowing them to under price our organization.	$15 million	Moderate

By completing an information-valuing exercise, the organization has a better understanding of what their information's value is to them. This is a key aspect to winning support for the establishment of the appropriate security controls within the organization's enterprise information systems.

If you are protecting an information asset worth $5 billion, it would be a far more defendable position to establish security controls that will cost the organization $10 million. However, if the information asset is only worth $500,000, a $10 million expenditure may most likely not be warranted.

Security control selection

Now that you have completed the activity of information categorization, found your organizational information assets, discovered where your organizational information is located within the information system, organized your information into discrete protection categories, and assigned a dollar value to your information you are in an excellent position to begin establishing the security controls necessary to protect your organization's information. You have worked with the business and IT teams to establish the importance of the data within your organization. You can use this information to architect the needed security controls for the information system.

Prior to establishing the security controls for your information systems, you must look at your organization's regulatory and compliance requirements to make sure that you are building a security framework that ensures you are complying.

As you are in the process of building your organization's framework you should review the security frameworks that are already in existence:

- Many of the frameworks exist to solve a compliance requirement. Using these frameworks will help to make sure you are going in the right direction.
- Thousands of combined hours have gone into developing these security frameworks. It does not make any sense for you to start from scratch. Benefit yourself and your organization by utilizing one or more of these excellent security frameworks.
- Based on my experience, I recommend the use of the NIST Framework:
    - Map the NIST Framework to any other specific compliance requirements as needed based on your organizational compliance needs.

Information security frameworks

The following are a selection of information security frameworks that you can use to inform your security control selection decisions:

- **NIST CSF**: https://www.nist.gov/cyberframework
- **COBIT**: http://www.isaca.org/cobit/pages/default.aspx
- **ITIL**: https://www.axelos.com/best-practice-solutions/itil
- **NIST SP 800-53**: http://nvlpubs.nist.gov/nistpubs/SpecialPublications/NIST.SP.800-53r4.pdf
- **ISO 27002**: https://www.iso.org/standard/54533.html

- **COSO**: https://www.coso.org/Pages/default.aspx
- **NIST SP 800-171**: http://nvlpubs.nist.gov/nistpubs/SpecialPublications/ NIST.SP.800-171.pdf

Based on the analysis that you conducted as part of the information categorization step you will now be able to develop the baseline set of controls for your information system:

1. Apply the appropriate baseline set of controls based on the high watermark value derived from the information categorization step.
2. Tailor the controls that you have selected:
    - **Common controls**: You do always need to implement a security control in your environment. For example, if the network team has already implemented a specific control on your network you do not need to re-apply the control. You do however, need to ensure that the common control is in place and maintained as this common control ensures the security of your data.
    - **Scoping considerations**: Does a control baseline have a requirement for wireless networking? What if your information system does not implement wireless networking? This would be an example where you would scope out this requirement as it would not be applicable.
    - **Compensating controls**: You are not always able to implement a security control as intended. Sometimes implementing a security control will render the information system unusable. The implementation of compensating controls ensures that necessary security functionality is added to the information system that makes up for the loss of the security control that cannot be implemented.
    - **Additional security controls**: Your security control baseline may not be the only place that you are pulling security controls from. You may have additional compliance requirements depending on your organization's mission. You may have established controls that are specific to your organization. In this case, you add in these security controls now.
3. Develop a security control package for your information system that will be used to ensure the security controls are as follows:
    - Included as requirements, as part of information system planning
    - Architected as part of the system design
    - Integrated as part of system implementation
    - Tested as part of system acceptance
    - Monitored for the life of the system

NIST Special Publication 800-37 Revision 1, CHAPTER THREE, provides further guidance on the topic of security control selection at: `http://nvlpubs.nist.gov/nistpubs/SpecialPublications/NIST.SP.800-37r1.pdf`.

Security control implementation

Security control implementation is where the rubber meets the road for all of the effort that has been conducted regarding information categorization and security control selection with business and IT users. Security control implementation must be carefully planned and communicated with the project team that is implementing the new information system, ensuring that no information security control is left unimplemented.

Now that we are at the point in the system development life cycle where we are working to develop the information system, we must ensure that the project's scope includes the security control implementation as part of the overall project scope. While the information security professional will play an important role in the implementation of the security controls, this will be a team effort. Security controls must be assigned to the appropriate IT team member to ensure that that the correct subject matter expert is involved.

You should work to categorize your security controls so that you can more easily provide the controls to the subject matter experts for implementation. As an example, controls related to network security will not typically be implemented by your web applications team. Following are some categories that you can split your security controls into so that you can more easily manage them with your IT teams:

- **Physical and environmental**: Electrical, data center, physical access, and environmental
- **Documentation categories**: User rules for behavior, requirements documents, configuration management plan, design document, and IT contingency plan
- **Roles**: Chief information officer, chief information security officer, ISSO, system administrator, application developer, network engineering, project manager, information security, and application administrator
- **Technical Controls**: Access controls, collaborative computing, wireless, encryption, account management, auditing, authentication, DMZ, disaster recovery, mobile devices, VoIP, servers, and workstation

The information security professional must ensure that they are able to fully support the rest of the technical team during the implementation of information security controls in order to ensure that the controls are adequately implemented.

Assessing implemented security controls

The goal of assessing the implemented security controls is to ensure that the controls have been adequately implemented as part of the information system.

In order to properly assess the information system's security controls you should be asking if the security controls are the following:

- **Implemented as expected**: Are the agreed upon security control designs part of the production information system?
- **Operating appropriately**: Are the security controls impacting the production system negatively and providing the required security functionality?

Testing security controls should be a formalized procedure within your organization. Security control implementation can be very complicated and there are typically a large number of requirements that need to be implemented. Without a formalized plan, you will find it very difficult to adequately and completely test your newly implemented security controls. Your testing procedures will be ad hoc, and you run the risk of missing important details.

The key activities that are part of the security control assessment phase are as follows:

- **Develop a security control assessment plan**: A specific plan should be developed that addresses how you will conduct the assessment including:
    - What requirements will be tested?
    - What procedures will be used to conduct the tests?
    - What tools will be used to conduct testing?
- **Execute the security control assessment plan**: Execute the previously developed plan against the production information system.
- **Develop the security assessment report**: Based on your findings from the security control assessment document, develop the following:
    - **Weaknesses**: Specific security-related issues that adversely affect the overall security posture of the information system
    - **Recommendations**: Information that guides the subject matter expert in mitigating the finding
- **Remediate and reassess weaknesses**: Mitigate weaknesses based on the security assessment report. Reassess after a weakness has been mitigated to ensure that the issue has been closed.

NIST Special Publication 800-37 Revision 1 provides further guidance on the topic of security control Assessment at: `http://nvlpubs.nist.gov/nistpubs/SpecialPublications/NIST.SP.800-37r1.pdf`

Authorizing information systems to operate

Now that you have tested your information systems' security controls, validating that the controls have been effectively implemented and that they are operating as expected, it is now time to prepare for the system to be approved for production use.

This step in the process is referred to as system authorization. The purpose of this step is to allow an officially designated senior leader within the organization to decide whether an information system will be approved for production use, or whether a current operating system can continue to be used.

An authorizing official has options when it comes to deciding how they will treat a system that is requesting to operate on the production network.

The authorizing official can do the following:

- Authorize the system to operate:
    - In this case, the authorizing official approves the system based on the evidence provided, and allows the system to go to production
    - The system may have one or more **Plan of Actions and Milestones (POAM)** associated with it, which are deficiencies that need to be mitigated

POAMs are not just the identification of weaknesses in an IT system. The purpose of a POAM is to set:

- Clear milestones to remediate a weakness and
- To establish clear funding for the remediation activities

This information allows the authorizing officials to make informed decisions about work that is still left to be completed on an IT system, and what the plan is to close out this work:

- In this case, the authorizing official has accepted the risk associated with the POAMs and their expected schedule for remediation
- Does not authorize the system to operate/remediate any deficiencies:
    - In this case, the authorizing official chooses not to immediately authorize the system
    - The IT team is instructed to go back and close out POAMs that are deemed to be high risk
    - Once those POAMs are closed out the IT team can return back to the authorizing official with a new request
    - An authorizing official may choose to require all POAMs to be remediated or a subset of the total POAMs
    - As this is a risk-based decision on the part of a senior leader it will depend on the decision of the specific authorizing official

The steps associated with achieving authorization are as follows:

1. Develop your plan of actions and millstones based on the security assessment report:
    - You do not need to include any remediated activities as part of the POAMs since you have already fixed any uncovered weaknesses
    - There is nothing wrong with letting your approving official know that you did uncover weaknesses and that they have been mitigated
2. Assemble the security authorization package for your authorizing official to review:
    1. You will need to work with your authorizing official to determine what they would like to see in their authorization package and how they would like to see it
    2. As mentioned earlier, this depends on the individual authorizing official
    3. Minimum items you should expect to include are as follows:
        - Failed tests from the security assessment report
        - Plan of actions and milestones

- Statement of residual risk:
  - This document provides the authorization official with the recommendation from an information security perspective regarding risk to reputation, IT operations, and mission

4. Authorization decision document

NIST Special Publication 800-37 Revision 1 provides additional guidance regarding authorizing information systems at: `http://nvlpubs.nist.gov/nistpubs/ SpecialPublications/NIST.SP.800-37r1.pdf`

Monitoring information system security controls

Now that we have a production information system that has been fully authorized to operate by an executive leader with the appropriate authority to accept risk on the behalf of the organization, we now need to begin the process of operations and maintenance.

The operations and management phase for an information system is referred to as continuous monitoring. The purpose behind continuous monitoring is to ensure that the security controls that where designed and tested as part of the information system's development continue to be effective over the life of the system.

In the past, an information security professional would ensure that an information system was adequately protected as it was going into production. After that, the system was treated as secure until the authorizing official or compliance requirements dictated it was time to review the security documentation again. The reality is that an information system does not stay secure for very long if you are not paying careful attention.

Some factors that erode an information system's security are as follows:

- **The need to patch**: New vulnerabilities are discovered all the time
- **Changes to the system**: A new change, whether it is a new server service, web application, or office automation tool could bring a new weakness and therefore risk to the organization
- **Changes in technology**: A best practice today may not be a best practice tomorrow
- **Path of least resistance**: To meet customer expectations, system operators may take shortcuts in information security

You will want to establish a program that ensures you have good visibility into your organization's information systems from a security perspective, in order to ensure the continued security of those information systems.

Some mechanisms to continuously monitor information systems are as follows:

- **Configuration management**:
    - **Tools**: These types of tools allow the operations team to effectively monitor changes to information system settings:
        1. A configuration management tool is a necessity in a modern enterprise to manage the many settings in a modern information system
        2. These tools should also allow for the appropriate security control baseline to be applied and reapplied if it is removed without authorization
    - **Process**: A robust change management system should be in place allowing stakeholders to discuss changes to the information system and determine potential risk to the information system and the organization
- **Vulnerability management tools**: These tools can be used to identify changes in configuration from the security baselines, as well as new vulnerabilities that may occur over time due to newly discovered flaws in technology.
- **Patch management tools**: These tools work to ensure that new patches required by the information system are available and automatically installed on the system. Key points to remember are as follows:
    - Not all patches will install properly. Sometimes manual intervention is required.
    - Not all information systems are supported by patch management systems. Sometimes you will need to monitor the software distribution news for your vendor. If they post a security patch you should manually download and install the patch.
- **Asset management tools**: These tools serve to ensure that new devices added to the network or information system are cataloged as part of a detailed asset inventory.
- **Periodic audits**: For those items that cannot be easily tested via automation you will need to develop procedures to ensure that those controls are tested periodically.

Calculating risk

In this section, we will look at the difference between qualitative and quantitative risk assessments.

Qualitative risk analysis

A qualitative risk assessment is based on an individual's perception regarding the probability that a particular risk may occur at a given time, and whether that risk will have a genuine impact on the organization. The key thing to understand about qualitative risk assessments is that they do not utilize any mathematical calculation method to calculate a certain risk. As a result, qualitative risk analysis is relatively easy to perform and is typically the type of risk assessment that is performed by the information security professional.

The qualitative risk assessment provides a method where the information security professional can rank risk on a subjective scale as seen in the following, where risk is ranked high, medium, or low.

Qualitative risk assessments are not as precise as quantitative risk assessments as they do not contain a mathematical component, where you are taking non-subjective risk data to build a numerical score. However qualitative risk assessments are generally favored as they are less expensive to conduct, can be accomplished rapidly, and produce the information necessary for organizational leadership to make a decision rapidly.

Identifying your organizations threats

When conducting a qualitative risk assessment, the first thing you will do is develop a list of threats that your organization is likely to encounter. You will want to develop a list that at a minimum includes the following:

- **Threat**: Any circumstance or event with the potential to adversely impact organizational operations (including mission, functions, image, or reputation), organizational assets, individuals, other organizations, or the nation through an information system through unauthorized access, destruction, disclosure, or modification of information, and/or denial of service
- **Threat source**: The intent and method targeted at the intentional exploitation of a vulnerability, or a situation and method that may accidentally exploit a vulnerability

- **Description**: A short narrative that defines the threat / threat source pairing, helping to ensure a uniform application of this information throughout the risk management process:

Threat	Threat source	Threat description
Storage failure	Structural (IT equipment)	Storage critical to your organization's operations ceases to function causing a disruption in your organization's operations.
Internet outage	Structural (IT equipment)	An internet outage occurs causing a disruption in communication between customers, business partners, and critical applications.
Insider threat	Human	A trusted user within your organization uses their knowledge of the organization to circumvent technical security controls and organizational policy in order to harm the organization.
Insider threat privileged user	Human	Similar to the preceding example, however in this case the user has elevated privileges on the information system allowing them to have a greater negative impact on the organization.
External hacking	Human	An external user or organization targets your organization in order to exfiltrate sensitive information, or to cause a disruption in your organization's operations.
Flood	Natural disaster	A flood event occurs that disrupts your organization's operations.
Fire	Natural disaster	A fire event occurs that disrupts your organization's operations.
Hurricane	Natural disaster	A hurricane event occurs that disrupts your organization's operations.

Now that we have gone through the exercise of identifying threats, we need to conduct further analysis to see if we have an active threat source that is able to carry out the threat against our organization.

A valid threat source is characterized as follows:

- A source that targets your organization to exploit a vulnerability
- A situation where a vulnerability may be accidentally exploited

Considering this, you would now analyze your list of threats and determine if any of these threats meet these criteria. For the purposes of our example, we will determine that a flood or hurricane are not threats to our environment due to our geographic location. Our remaining threats are still valid in our example as we have determined that they could be specifically targeted or could be accidentally exploited.

Identifying your organizations vulnerabilities

The next step in the risk assessment process is to identify the vulnerabilities in your information systems. In order to conduct a thorough review of the information system you will need to examine multiple sources of information and utilize varied testing methods.

Information sources:

- **Business team**: Work with your business users to understand how they conduct their activities. You may find some vulnerabilities in the underlying information systems by asking how they conduct their day:
    - Do your business users access a business-critical system while teleworking without VPN or strong access controls?
- **IT team**: Work with the IT team to understand how operations run and how information systems are configured:
    - Do the development team's test and development environments have unfettered internet access?
    - Change control:
        - Are changes to the production information system passed through a change control board?
        - Are those changes reviewed and approved by all stakeholders including security?
- **Technical tools**: Utilize technical security tools to discover and validate vulnerabilities on the network:
    - Network vulnerability scanning
    - Web application vulnerability scanning
    - Source code vulnerability scanner

- **Third-party auditing and testing**: Utilize the services of third-party auditors and testers to discover the vulnerabilities within your information system:
  - **Compliance auditing and testing**: Utilize a third party to inspect your information system for compliance with organizational compliance standards. These types of audits should include a vulnerability assessment.
  - **Vulnerability assessment**: Have a third party inspect your organization for vulnerabilities.

It is a best practice from an information security program perspective to have periodic external vulnerability assessments. A mature information security program will help conduct vulnerability assessments as part of continuously monitoring the environment. However, having a third party come in on a periodic basis will help to ensure that your information security program is discovering and reporting on all vulnerabilities.

  - **Penetration test**: A much more intensive test than a vulnerability assessment. A penetration test takes the results of vulnerability assessment and tests the information system to see if the specific device is exploitable.

As you conduct your vulnerability assessment, ensure that you capture information related to your testing so that you can go back to the information source if there are future questions:

Vulnerabilities discovered	Point of contact	Method of discovery
Storage mechanisms utilized are not redundant	Storage team	Interviewed team member and observed configuration. Artifact exists in the form of a configuration screenshot.
Single provider for internet access is utilized	Network team	Interviewed team member and observed configuration. Artifact exists in the form of a configuration screenshot and services contract.

Vulnerabilities discovered	Point of contact	Method of discovery
No mechanism exists to monitor user behavior on the information system	Systems team	Interviewed team member and observed configuration. Documented that there is no mechanism in place to conduct user behavior analytics.
No mechanism for privileged access management exists	Systems team	Interviewed team member and observed configuration. Documented that there is no mechanism in place to enforce privileged access management.
Development and test servers have been placed on the internet and forgotten	Development team external penetration team	Interviewed team member and observed configuration. Artifact exists in the form of a penetration test report and concurrence by development team.
Wet pipe sprinkler in data center	Facilities team	Interviewed team members. Artifact exists in the form of design information obtained from the facilities team.

Pairing threats with vulnerabilities

Now that you have established your information security vulnerabilities, it is time to begin pairing your vulnerabilities with the threats previously defined.

A threat without a vulnerability does not pose a risk to the organization. The inverse of this is also true in that a vulnerability without a threat does not pose a risk. The key is to establish your threat and vulnerability pairings so that you can identify what vulnerabilities your organization has that can be paired with valid threats. It is a valid pairing that generates risk for your organization, and this exercise allows you to identify what risks need to be addressed.

In the following example, we have taken the vulnerabilities and threats identified in the previous example and paired them appropriately.

We now need to perform further analysis:

Vulnerability	Threat	Threat source
Storage mechanisms utilized are not redundant.	Storage failure	Structural (IT equipment)
Single provider for internet access is utilized.	Internet outage	Structural (IT equipment)
No mechanism exists to monitor user behavior on the information system.	Insider threat	Human
No mechanism for privileged access management exists.	Insider threat privileged user	Human
Development and test servers have been placed on the internet and forgotten.	External hacking	Human
Wet pipe sprinkler in data center	Fire	Natural disaster

Estimating likelihood

Now that we have valid threat and vulnerability pairs, we now need to determine the likelihood that a given vulnerability will be acted upon by a threat source.

As you develop your information security program, the estimation of likelihood in this scenario should be a well-established repeatable process. While you can have multiple categories for likelihood, I recommend that you use only three (low, medium, and high). Using three categories keeps things simple and allows you to make a simpler decision, quicker decisions means you can move on to the real task of securing your organization. Ultimately, how many categories you use is dependent on your organizational culture and policies. Be careful when you start moving beyond three as people tend to start fighting over small points rather than the real issue.

A three-category likelihood scenario is defined as follows:

- **High**: The threat source is highly capable and motivated. The security controls in place are ineffective.
- **Medium**: The threat source is capable and motivated. The security controls in place may impede the successful exploitation of the vulnerability.
- **Low**: The threat source is not capable or motivated. Security controls are in place that impede the successful exploitation of the vulnerability.

Estimating impact

The impact that an organization may experience is the level of disruption that the organization expects because of the following:

- Unauthorized modification of information
- Theft of information
- Unauthorized destruction of information
- Loss of information system availability

This loss can be experienced throughout the organization as a whole, or can be directed at a specific business unit. It is important to make a careful assessment of business impact as things may not be as they seem if you rush through the process. An impact to the entire organization may not cause as large of an impact compared to something that happens within a specific business unit.

As an example, the organization may be able to reasonably tolerate a loss of availability of the corporate network due to contingency plans that are in place, even though it affects the entire organization. However, the loss of a single file that contains highly valuable intellectual property could cause an organization to lose business and could lead to the organization's eventual closure.

As with likelihood, we must define how we will measure impact. As with the previous example of likelihood, I recommend the use of three categories (low, medium, and high)

- **High**: The event is expected to have multiple, severe or catastrophic adverse effects on organizational operations, and/or assets
- **Medium**: The event is expected to have a serious adverse effect on organizational operations, and/or assets
- **Low**: The event is expected to have a limited adverse effect on organizational operations, and/or assets

Potential organizational impacts include the following:

- Financial loss
- Harm to individuals
- Damage to organizational assets
- Loss of operating capability

Conducting the risk assessment

Now that we have developed our lists of threats and vulnerabilities, and developed our rules on how we measure likelihood and impact, we are able to analyze risk. We will use the following risk assessment matrix utilizing the likelihood and impact rules developed previously:

		Impact		
		Low	Medium	High
Probability	Low	Low Risk	Low Risk	Medium Risk
	Medium	Low Risk	Medium Risk	High Risk
	High	Medium Risk	High Risk	High Risk

We will take the threat and vulnerability pairs table that we developed previously and include the likelihood, impact, and risk ratings from the preceding table:

Vulnerability	Threat	Threat Source	Likelihood	Impact	Risk Rating
Storage mechanisms utilized are not redundant.	Storage failure	Structural (IT equipment)	Low	High	Medium
Single provider for internet access is utilized.	Internet outage	Structural (IT equipment)	Medium	Medium	Medium
No mechanism exists to monitor user behavior on the information system.	Insider threat	Human	Low	Medium	Low
No mechanism for privileged access management exists.	Insider threat Privileged user	Human	Low	High	Medium
Development and test servers have been placed on the internet and forgotten.	External hacking	Human	High	High	High
Wet pipe sprinkler in data center	Fire	Natural disaster	Low	Medium	Low

Now that we have completed the risk assessment table, you can clearly see that priorities have bubbled up to the surface and that we have a clear priority to work from, regarding addressing risk:

- **High risk**: Development and rest servers have been placed on the internet and forgotten
- **Medium risk**:
  - No mechanism for privileged access management exists
  - Single provider for internet access is utilized
  - Storage mechanisms utilized are not redundant
- **Low risk**:
  - No mechanism exists to monitor user behavior on the information system
  - Wet pipe sprinkler in data center

Management choices when it comes to risk

When it comes to addressing risk, there is no simple answer. There are four ways that an organization can choose to respond to a newly discovered risk.

The organization can choose to do the following:

- **Mitigate risk**: Mitigation involves fixing the issue that is causing a vulnerability or implementing a compensating security control if the specific issue cannot be resolved.

  For example, good patching is a key component of any well-functioning IT organization. If a missing patch causes a vulnerability, then you would patch the system to mitigate the vulnerability. However, there are often IT devices that must be on the enterprise network and cannot be regularly patched due to vendor limitations or compliance requirements (for example, point of sale systems and healthcare devices). In environments where regular patching cannot be conducted, the devices in question must be tightly controlled through network segmentation and monitored by your organization's security operations center. These mitigating controls can allow these vulnerable devices to continue operating:

- **Transfer risk**: Transferring risk involves purchasing insurance to reduce the financial burden of a vulnerability being exercised by a threat source.

While information security insurance is currently a booming industry, there are some important points to note.

In order to get insurance, you need to demonstrate you are exercising due diligence and care regarding your information security responsibilities. Many questions will be asked when you start working with an insurance company to develop a policy. In short, you cannot use insurance to implement foundational security controls.

Standard business information security policies are beginning to explicitly exclude information security incidents. If you think you are covered, you may not be. Check with your provider.

- **Accept risk**: Accepting risk comes into play when a specific vulnerability you are trying to close costs more than the asset you are trying to fix. In this case, executive leadership may decide that the specific risk will be accepted and that the vulnerability in question will not be closed.

Accepting risk is where the concept of risk ownership needs to be highlighted again. Accepting risk is the responsibility of executive leadership, and not the IT team. The best, most cost-friendly plan that the IT organization can formulate should be developed and presented to management. If management chooses to not mitigate the risk that is their right. The IT team should not be making the decision to accept risk for management.

- **Avoiding risk**: By avoiding risk, the organization is choosing to not engage in the behavior that is causing the risk. In this example, the organization may choose to remove a vulnerable server from the internet until it is patched.

While risk avoidance is certainly an option, it is not one that will be typically exercised. It is a difficult call for management to remove a required business system from the network. When avoidance is used it may be for less critical functions.

Quantitative analysis

Quantitative analysis focuses on irrefutable data that can be measured versus the qualitative assessment, which is based on the opinions of the individuals conducting the assessment. The quantitative assessment performs mathematical calculations to express risk in terms of financial loss, which is very useful when working to seek acceptance from business leaders for financial support of an information security initiative.

Quantitative assessment has the benefit of being based on measurable data, which can greatly help the information security professional in delivering a precise risk score based on mission-specific information derived from your organization business units. Being expressed in terms of money, it makes it easier for your organization's executive leadership to determine the following:

- What would the cost be per year for a given risk?
- Is a given security control worth the cost, considering the cost of the risk exposure?

To conduct a quantitative risk assessment, you will need to understand a few new concepts and gather information from your organization related to these concepts as follows:

- **Single Loss Expectancy (SLE)**: Money that the organization will lose if a specific incident occurs one time:
    - **Asset value**: A factor of SLE. The value of the asset to the organization
    - **Exposure factor**: Another factor of SLE. The amount of loss that will occur to the asset value because of a threat
- **Annual Rate of Occurrence (ARO)**: The number of times that a specific incident is expected to occur within the organization
- **Annual Loss Expectancy (ALE)**: Once you understand your SLE and ARO, the annual loss expectancy is the money that your organization would expect to lose over a single year

ALE is the risk value associated with the qualitative assessment.

Qualitative risk assessment example

The following is an example of how to perform a qualitative risk assessment. You can use this example in your own organization by replacing the values in the book with your own:

1. First determine your threat, vulnerability, and risk:
   - **Threat**: Loss of customer information
   - **Vulnerability**: Web application vulnerabilities
   - **Risk**: Loss of information
2. Determine the **Asset Value (AV)**:
   - **AV** = $200,000.00
   - You should work with your business units when developing the assets value. The loss of data will mean something different to an IT user, a business user, and information security user.
3. Determine the **Exposure Factor (EF)**:
   - **EF** = 1.0
   - 100% = 1.0
   - In this case, the organization determined that a loss of this information is mission-critical and would result in a total loss resulting in an exposure factor of 100%
4. Now determine SLE:
   - **SLE** = AV X EF
   - $200,000 = $200,000 x 1.0
5. Now determine ARO:
   - **ARO** = .5
   - 1/2 = 50% = .5
   - An ARO has been estimated to represent an occurrence of once every two years
6. Now determine ALE:
   - ALE = SLE * ARO
   - $100,000 = $200,000 x .5
   - The organization has an annual risk of losing $100,000 if the organization loses their customers' information
   - This allows the organization to understand that if they spend less than the ALE to protect this information they are still making a good investment

The issue with the quantitative approach is as follows:

- Information may not be readily available to perform the assessment:
    - The organization may be too immature to understand that their data has value
    - The business users may not have a good grasp regarding what their asset values are
- The quantitative approach is much slower

A good approach is to combine both the qualitative and quantitative approaches:

- Utilize the qualitative risk assessment approach to quickly determine relevant risks within the organization
- Use the quantitative risk assessment approach to drill down into relevant risks in order to develop greater justification for risk mitigation

Summary

In this chapter, we learned about information security risk management and how to perform the necessary task of risk management, which can be applied to your organization.

We discussed the following:

- Information security risk management concepts and how they are applied to the organization
- How to determine where valuable information is located within your organization
- How to perform a quick initial risk assessment to determine an organization's health
- How risk management affects the organization
- How information categorization is performed
- How information security risk management is performed

In the next chapter, we will discuss how to develop your information security plan, which is the foundational component of establishing your information security program and its continued governance.

5

Developing Your Information and Data Security Plan

In this chapter, you will learn about the concepts necessary to develop your information security program plan. Your program plan will be a foundational document that will establish how your information security program will function and interact with the rest of the business.

In this chapter you will learn:

- How to develop the objectives for your information security program
- Elements of a successful information security program
- Business/mission alignment
- Information security program plan
- Establishing information security program enforcement

Determine your information security program objectives

When you begin the work to establish your information security program plan, you must take the time to reflect on what your objectives are for the program. It is not enough to say that you are going to secure things. You must understand the culture and maturity level of your organization and allow this to guide you in the development of your plan.

For instance, if your organization is very immature and conducts business and operations in a very ad hoc manner, you will find it very difficult to institute a program that starts off requiring rigorous policies and procedures to be followed. Instead, you must meet your organization where they are at delivering security services that meet the current need while planning for more sophisticated services as the organization matures.

Regardless of the maturity of your organization, there is typically always room to make improvements. As a result, when you begin your planning process you should break down your thought process into short-term and long-term activities.

Example information security program activities

Does the information security program have a charter that clearly defines the information security program's role within the organization?

- This is the document that establishes the authority of the information security program. If it does not exist, it must be created.
- It needs to be presented and agreed upon by your organization's executive team.
- It should be signed by a current executive within the organization. This individual should have significant authority across the entire organization.

Foundational information security activities (cyber/IT hygiene):

- **Discover assets**: Determine what assets are on your network
- **Secure configurations**: Implement best practice security
- **Restrict privileges**: Restrict administrative privileges to only the users that require them
- **Patching**: Ensure that information system patching is a high priority
- **Third-party management**: Ensuring that your vendors and suppliers are managing their information system in a secure manner
- **Training and awareness**: Training all of your organization users in their specific information security role
- **Framework selection**: Establish which frameworks your organization will follow
- **Information security metrics**: Establish metrics so that you can effectively report risks to your board and executives

While these foundational activities should be addressed immediately, they can be highly complex to implement. Also, there is a continuous monitoring component to these foundational activities. While you may need to implement a project to fix patching issues, your organization will never get to a point where your information systems do not need to be patched. In this example, patching will move from being a tracked project to an operations and management activity tracked by the information security program as an ongoing continuous monitoring program activity.

The following image summarizes the foundational information security activities:

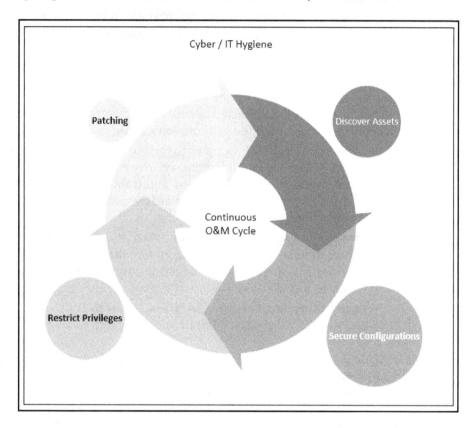

Elements for a successful information security program

The following are the elements for a successful information security program:

- **Policy**: The rules for how your information security program behaves in addition to organizational policy
- **Information security services**: Technical and operational capabilities provided to the organization as a service:
    - Vulnerability management service (vulnerability scanners)
    - Malware detection services (antivirus/anti-malware)
    - Log monitoring services (SIEM/log aggregation)
    - Threat detection services (host and network IDs)
- **Security architecture**: Working with the business and IT teams to ensure that new IT systems are properly architected to properly protect the information that they contain commensurate with the information's value
- **Information security guidance**: Working with the business and IT teams helping them to properly understand and implement security requirements:
    - **Information security awareness and training**: Specific training where information system users are trained in the acceptable use of the information system
    - **Information security advisement**: Activities implemented by the information security program to ensure that information security requirements are properly understood and implemented by both business and IT users
    - **Information security categorization**: Assist the business and IT users in the proper categorization of information assets

These information security program functions provide the organization's management, operational, and technical information security controls which, when properly implemented, work to secure the organization-sensitive information:

- **Technical controls**: Security controls implemented on the information system that serve to protect the information system from unauthorized access. These are controls that are installed and reside on the information system by the IT team. Examples of technical controls include:
    - **Firewalls**: Devices that restrict network traffic into and out of a network zone.

- **Encryption**: Can be used to protect data in motion as well as data at rest by protecting the confidentiality of data:
  - For data in motion you may implement a protocol such as **IPSec** to protect data being transmitted from one server to another.
  - For data at rest you could implement a tool such as BitLocker on a Microsoft Windows system. This tool serves to ensure that data on a hard drive is kept confidential if the hard disk is stolen.
- **Antivirus software**: Provides protection against malware infections. Can be implemented at the server, workstation or network level.

- **Operational controls**: Security controls that are implemented on an ongoing basis by individuals within the organization. Many of these control types deal with the day-to-day operations of the organizational information systems. Examples of operational controls include:
  - **Contingency planning**: A process where an organization establishes how it will respond to a system outage
  - **Configuration management**: The utilization of organizational-approved baselines to ensure a common configuration across devices
  - **Change management**: A process where organizational stakeholders review proposed changes to document that a change is occurring and to ascertain whether potential misconfigurations may exist in the change

- **Management controls**: Policies, practices, and procedures at the organizational, information system, and personnel levels. Examples of management controls include:
  - **Vulnerability assessment**: An assessment by an information security professional that attempts to uncover weaknesses in an information system. The vulnerability assessment will be reconducted as weaknesses are mitigated to ensure that the weakness no longer exists.
  - **Penetration tests**: Penetration tests take the output of the vulnerability assessment and attempt to exploit the weaknesses that were discovered.

It is very common to see vulnerability assessments improperly categorized as penetration tests by information security professionals. A penetration test is a much deeper dive into the information system than a vulnerability assessment and requires a much more skilled information security professional than a vulnerability assessment requires.

This difference between penetration tests and vulnerability assessments is important for many reasons:

- Penetration tests cost more than vulnerability assessments
- Penetration tests examine the information system much more closely
- Penetration tests remove false positives from the vulnerability assessment

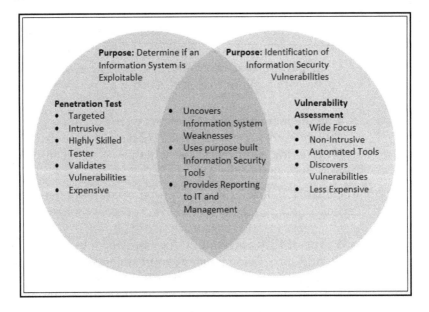

- **Risk assessments**: Quantitative and qualitative risk assessments that serve to inform management regarding the risk to their information and information systems.

The organization's information security program utilizes a layered approach (defense in depth) to ensure adequate protection of sensitive information across the enterprise network:

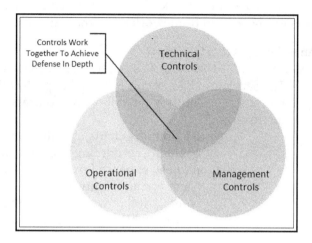

Analysis to rightsizing your information security program

Rightsizing your information security program ensures that your program is properly aligned with the needs of your organization. As you are developing your plans to build out your information security program, you should look at a few key data points that will help you in establishing your business-focused information security requirements.

Compliance requirements

The compliance requirements that an organization needs to follow will have great effect on the overall shaping of the information security program that will be planned and implemented. The requirements imposed by various laws and compliance frameworks vary from law to framework, and it is critically important that you understand your framework to ensure that your organization can successfully continue to do business.

Without understanding your organization's legal requirements, you run the very real risk of your organization being hit with very serious fines or even being shut down. The following list shows some examples of legal frameworks that are imposed upon organizations, some of the key requirements for those legal frameworks, and the organizations that are affected:

- **The Sarbanes-Oxley Act (SOX), 2002**
  (`https://www.gpo.gov/fdsys/pkg/PLAW-107publ204/content-detail.html`):
  - The Sarbanes-Oxley Act is intended to protect the public and investors by requiring reliability and accuracy of financial disclosures:
    - **Key requirements**: Auditor independence, public company accounting oversight, analyst conflicts of interest, enhanced financial disclosures, corporate fraud accountability, corporate responsibility, commission resources and authority, corporate tax returns, white-collar crime penalty enhancements, corporate and criminal fraud accountability, and studies and reports.
    - **Who is impacted?** US public companies and public accounting firms.

- **Payment Card Industry Data Security Standard: PCI DSS**
  (`https://www.pcisecuritystandards.org/document_library?document=pci_ds s`):
  - PCI DSS is a set of requirements established to enhance the security of customer payment card data. The standard was developed by the *PCI Security Standards Council*. The council includes members from Discover Financial Services, American Express, MasterCard Worldwide, Visa, and JCB International:
    - **Key Requirements**: Maintain an information security policy, operations and maintenance of applications and systems must be secure, physical access to cardholder data must be restricted, IDs for computer access must be unique, network resources and cardholder data access must be tracked and monitored, information security tools, controls, and processes must be regularly tested, cardholder data must be encrypted across unencrypted public networks, where cardholder data exists to operate and maintain firewalls, access to cardholder data should be restricted on a need-to-know basis, cardholder data should be protected at rest, security

parameters and system password defaults must be changed to improve security, and use and maintain antivirus software.

- **Who is impacted**? Credit card companies, retailers, and any other entity that handles payment card information.

- **The Gramm-Leach-Bliley Act (GLB), 1999** (`https://www.ftc.gov/tips-advice/business-center/guidance/how-comply-privacy-consumer-financial-information-rule-gramm`) and (`https://www.ftc.gov/tips-advice/business-center/privacy-and-security/gramm-leach-bliley-act`):
    - The GLB Act serves to protect consumer personal financial information held by financial institutions:
        - **Key requirements**: Financial privacy rule, safeguards rule, and pretexting provisions
        - **Who is impacted**? Securities firms, insurance companies, banks, brokers, lenders, and other financial institutions

- **Electronic Fund Transfer Act, 1978** (`https://www.fdic.gov/regulations/laws/rules/6500-3100.html`):
    - The law was established to protect consumers that utilize electronic fund transfers from errors and fraud:
        - **Key requirements**: Defining access devices (for example, debit cards), acceptance of device by the consumer, responsibilities of the financial institution, rights and responsibilities of the consumer, processes for error resolution, and electronic check transaction and preauthorized debit rules.
        - **Who is impacted**: Merchants and financial institutions that provide EFT services or manage consumer accounts.

- **Fair and Accurate Credit Transaction Act (FACTA), 2003**
  (`https://www.ftc.gov/enforcement/rules/rulemaking-regulatory-reform-pr oceedings/fair-credit-reporting-act`):
    - The law was established to protect consumers from identity fraud:
        - **Key requirements**: Ability to obtain a free credit report once a month, establishment of fraud alerts, payment card data truncation in financial files, victim access to financial fraud information, victim protection from collection agencies, financial institutions must implement early warning fraud detection mechanisms, consumer report information must be properly disposed, and consumer credit information disputing mechanisms.
        - **Who is impacted**? Financial institutions, credit reporting agencies, credit bureaus, and creditors.

- **Federal Information Security Management Act (FISMA), 2002**
  (`http://csrc.nist.gov/drivers/documents/FISMA-final.pdf`):
    - The law requires federal agencies to develop information security program and to safeguard their information and information systems:
        - **Key requirements**: Develop policies and procedures, conduct periodic tests of information security controls, conduct periodic risk assessments, develop information security plans, conduct security awareness training, respond to information security incidents, and ensure continuity of operations of information systems.
        - **Who is impacted**? Federal agencies.

- **Health Insurance Portability and Accountability Act (HIPAA), 1996**
  (`https://www.hhs.gov/hipaa/`):
    - The law requires that organizations adopt standards for securing patient health records as well as mechanisms for ensuring standardized identifiers for providers:

- **Key requirements**: Providers must use the same code sets and identifiers when doing business electronically. Federal protections are provided for personal health information under the control of a healthcare provider. Specific operational, management, and technical security controls required to safeguard personal health information. Providers, employers, and health plans have standard identifiers on medical transactions.
- **Who is impacted**? Health plans, health care providers, and organizations that manage personal health information.

- **European Union Data Protection Directive 1995** (http://ec.europa.eu/justice/data-protection/):
    - Establishes strict rules around the use of personal data:
        - **Key requirements**: Notice of data collection, data can only be used for its intended purpose, consent must be given to disclose data to a third party, information security must be maintained, individuals must be notified if their data is being collected, and individuals must be allowed to update their data.
        - **Who is impacted**? European businesses or non-European businesses that export data to another country.

As you can see, the requirements and industries vary greatly across the various legal frameworks. Additionally, this is a very small subset of the many laws around the world that speak to information data protection and the requirements imposed on an organization.

Something you will want to think about as you are looking at your organization's compliance requirements is whether you are sitting in multiple legal frameworks or whether you operate in multiple-industry sectors:

- It is not uncommon for organizations to accept credit cards today. You may be subject to PCI DSS:
    - Does your organization have a company store?
    - Do you manufacture items and sell them online?

- Does your organization exist in multiple sectors?
    - Is your organization a holding corporation?
        - Does your organization manufacture engines, run a hospital, and bake cookies?
        - These three sectors are wildly different and have very different information compliance requirements.
        - This means that your enterprise information security program must manage these unique requirements.

Is your organization centralized or decentralized?

An important aspect to information security program planning is determining whether your organization takes a centralized or decentralized approach to management and information technology.

Centralized

In a centrally managed organization, both policy and IT infrastructure are managed from a centralized program typically under a CIO as a shared service to the rest of the organization. The shared service environment typically provides most of the IT services for the entire organization. Subsidiary organizations may provide specialized IT functions specific to their missions. In this type of an environment, your information security program will:

- Interface with the shared services organization to secure enterprise shared services through enterprise policies
- Work with business users throughout the organization and IT to understand mission and information protection requirements
- Work within the individual organizational units to understand if there are specialized IT requirements that need to be addressed:
    - For example, manufacturing will have different IT requirements than HR, and thus will have specialized security requirements:

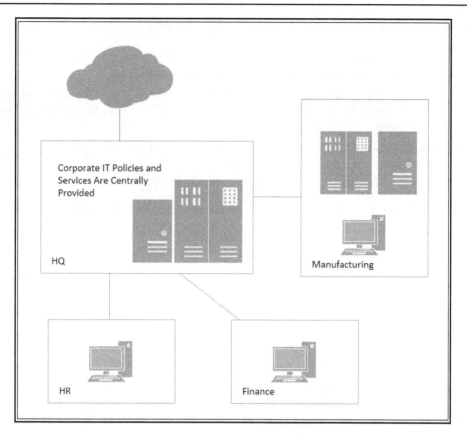

Decentralized

In a decentralized organization, individual organization units fully provide their own IT services or provide most of their IT services with supplementation from an enterprise shared service organization. The level of decentralization that an organization presents is highly dependent on the history and culture of the organization and how it has grown and changed over the years. In the following example, the **HR** and **Finance** groups receive shared services from the corporate service provider, while the manufacturing group provides its own IT services. The exception in this example is denoted by the dotted line. The dotted line represents a shared service of email that the corporate shared service provider has implemented for the entire company.

In this type of environment, your information security program will:

- Interface with the various organizations within your organization that provide IT, ensuring that common security policies are followed.
- Separations of corporate IT can be due to compliance requirements. Ensure that you fully understand the reason behind the multiple IT functions and plan accordingly.
- Business users may have different expectations of service depending on the culture of the organization unit. You will need to take these expectations into account as you plan your information security program:

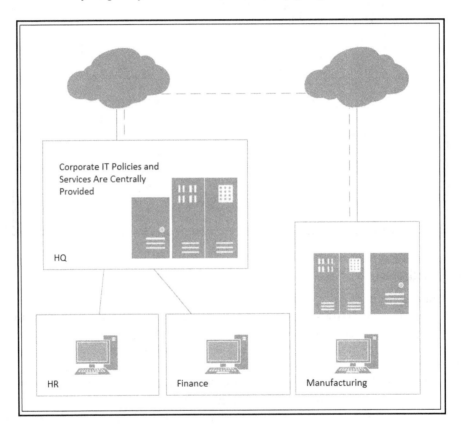

What is your organization's business risk appetite?

Risk appetite speaks to the level of risk tolerance your organization is willing to accept. There are two aspects to risk appetite that must be investigated:

- How much risk is your organization willing to tolerate?
- How much is your organization willing to spend to reduce risk?

Understanding your organization's risk appetite is a key element to building a successfully-sized information security program. If your organization has a very low risk appetite, then you will most likely have a very robust information security program designed to identify and mitigate risks to the lowest extent possible. Comparing this to an organization with a high-risk appetite, your organization may choose to not implement security counter measures in favor of risk acceptance.

Cyber risk appetite is a concept that is set by the senior most members of your organization (CEO, COO, and so on). It is important to understand that risk appetite is not a function to be determined within the IT organization. Risk appetite is not a technical concept. Rather, it is a management concept where key business leaders articulate what risk they are willing for the organization to bear and thus what information security controls should be implemented to reduce risk:

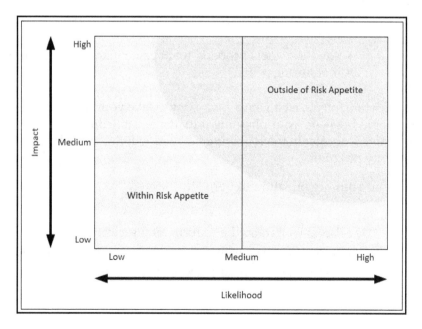

How mature is your organization?

The maturity of your organization will directly impact the progress that you will be able to make regarding the planning and implementation of your information security program.

In the following list, you will find some questions that will help you to think about your organization's current maturity. You will want to ask yourself similar questions to determine where you are staring from when planning your information security program.

Where is your organization now?

- **People**:
    - Does your organization have an existing information security capability? What is that capability?
    - Is this capability technical in nature only or does information security have a relationship with the business users?

- **Process**:
    - Is your organization's information security program chartered and supported by senior leadership?
    - Do you have organization-wide information security policies?

- **Technology**:
    - What information security tools has your organization implemented?
    - Are those tools properly management and is continuous monitoring active?

You will want to define for yourself where you want to take your information security program. You should break up your planning into manageable durations and chunks of work to avoid *boiling the ocean*. In the following list, you will find sample goals for an information security program.

Where do you want your organization to be?

- **First 90 days**:
    - Users well trained in information security principles
    - Information security is part of the decision-making process
    - Assessment of organizational risk conducted

- **Six months**:
    - Development and acceptance of information security policies
    - Information security is part of the system's development life cycle and change management process
- **Year one**:
    - Full adoption of information security policies
    - Repeatable information security metric reporting
    - Operation security—security tools, security operations center

Helping to guarantee success

Following are some guiding principles that you should use to help ensure that your information security program plan is well accepted by your organization.

Business alignment

A key success factor for a modern information security program is business alignment. I hope that you have noticed that I keep discussing this concept throughout the book. This is because it is so incredibly important for your success. An information security program that is well aligned with your business needs will be presenting solutions that the business wants in a way that the business understands. This is attained through careful interactions with your business users and ensuring that you follow the rule that you have one mouth and two ears so ensure that you listen twice as much as you speak. To help you better ensure business alignment:

- Collaborate with your business users often regarding information security topics that affect them
- Embed information security in the business decision making so that it becomes second nature
- Educate business leaders in their responsibilities regarding information security

Information security is a business project not an IT project

The information security program should be executed under the authority of the organization's business/mission leaders. An information security program that operates as an IT project is often viewed as a technology deployment. Rather than a well-aligned business project, organizational users will think the information security program is about deploying firewalls and intrusion detection systems. While these are very important tools, the information security program acts as an advocate between the business and IT, helping to ensure that the business's information security requirements are well articulated and implemented by IT.

Organizational change management

Communication is key to the successful implementation of an information security program. Ensuring that your users understand why the information security program is doing what it is doing is paramount.

Key communication concepts include:

- **Background**: Communicate to your organization the reason you are conducting an initiative:
    - Clearly develop your vision and communicate that vision to the organization
    - Provide a roadmap for where you are today and where you expect your organization to move to
- **Results**: What do you plan to achieve because of the change?
    - How will the day-to-day life of the organizational user change?
- **Plans**: Clearly communicate the plan associated with your changes to your organization:
    - Instill confidence in your organization by ensuring that your project plan is well communicated
- **Committee development**: Establish key stakeholder groups to ensure participations:
    - **Senior leadership**: A steering committee comprised of senior leadership will instill confidence and help to ensure that leadership has a say in the development and implementation of the security program

- **User group**: Having a user group of individuals from across the organization will serve to ensure that the usability of the information security program and its products is high

- **Marketing and communications**: Develop specific marketing/communication strategies targeted around the change:
    - **Senior leadership**: Should include:
        1. Develop materials that are easily digested and do not take longer than 30 seconds to read through
        2. Materials should not be in tech speak
        3. Materials should help senior leadership to understand that your change is aligned with and is helping to improve the organization's mission

    - **IT staff**: Should be technical in detail and include:
        1. Purpose and impact of change include technical detail
        2. Technical details of change
        3. How the new change will be measured and reported to management

    - **General users**: Should include:
        1. Purpose and impact of changes without technical details
        2. Ongoing communications around change status
        3. Clear change date with expectations and any responsibilities the user has in the change

Key information security program plan elements

Now that you have gathered the information needed to properly rightsize and establish the vision for your information security program, it is time to begin establishing your plan. The information security program plan is a management document for the information security professional to establish key decisions and planning information as it relates to the execution of the information security program.

Develop your information security program strategy

To ensure that you are developing a holistic business-aligned information security program, you need to take the time to establish an information security program strategy. You should establish clear and concise strategy goals that will help you in your future program planning.

Examples of strategic goals your organization can use include:

- **Information security risk assessment**: Provide for the periodic review of information security risks and implement appropriate responses
- **Information security governance**: Establish a governance function to provide information concerning information security assurance to management, assisting them in making decisions concerning risk
- **Information security operations**: Provide for proactive and reactive activities in response to penetration attempts
- **Information security architecture**: Support engineering and development teams in the secure development and implementation of information systems
- **Information security awareness and training**: Provide information on security awareness and training to personnel
- **Information security guidance**: Facilitate the protection of information systems and data by providing IT security policies, procedures, and supporting guidance

The information security program strategy statements that you develop should be used as a guide for any future project that you wish to implement in support of enterprise information security.

Establish key initiatives

The key initiatives that you define take your strategy and define it down further to tasks that you want to implement to improve the overall security of your organization. You still want to follow all previous guidance ensuring that you are aligning these initiatives with the needs of your organization.

The following example initiative can be used as a template for your information security program:

- **Initiative**: Security policy, standards, and guidelines framework.
- **Enables strategic goal**: Information security guidance—facilitate the protection of information systems and data by providing IT security policies, procedures, and supporting guidance.
- **Description**: Develop, approve, and implement information security policies, standards, and guidelines based on the standard for information security. These policies establish organization-wide responsibility for information protection.
- **Benefits**: The following are the benefits:
    - Established information security baseline for the entire organization
    - Repeatable implementation of information security controls across the enterprise
    - Information security policy that is established based on business need

Define roles and responsibilities

Establishing roles and responsibilities is very important to ensure a smooth planning process for the organization. These roles and responsibilities will be the ones that will be assigned specific information security functions in future policies and procedures.

Example roles and responsibilities you can include in your information security program plan include:

- **Executive management**: Executive managers are senior business managers who own the IT security risk for the organization and are responsible for overseeing information security for their respective areas of responsibility and ensuring compliance with all information security policies. Such responsibilities include, but are not limited to:
    - Ensure that the necessary funding required to provide adequate information security management for information systems under their control is acquired
    - Ensure that information security policies are adhered to within their respective area of responsibility

- Ensure that the data owner properly classifies data and that the information owner has properly established information security controls to protect that data
- Ensure that adequate training is budgeted for and provided to teams maintaining information systems

- **Chief information security officer**: The chief information security officer is responsible for operating and maintaining the enterprise-wide information security program, including:
    - Develops, documents, and disseminates organization-wide information security policies
    - Responsible for the information security risk management program
    - Establishes the information security training and awareness program
    - Provides guidance on how to implement enterprise information security policies
    - Manages the information security compliance programs
    - Establishes information security technical requirements, standards, and procedures
    - Authorizes exceptions to the information security policy

- **Data owner**: Data owners are responsible for ensuring that data under their responsibility is maintained in accordance with applicable organizational policies and governmental rules, laws, and regulations. Such responsibilities include, but are not limited to:
    - Identifies and classifies data under their control
    - Implements technical information security requirements to protect data
    - Establishes rules for data labeling:
        - Sensitive data
        - Confidential data
    - Establishes rules for how data should be accessed
    - Establishes rules for proper sanitization and disposal of data when the information system is decommissioned

- **System owner**: System owners are responsible for ensuring that information systems meet the requirements of the data owner in addition to applicable organizational policies and governmental rules, laws, and regulations. Such responsibilities include, but are not limited to:
    - Responsible for the successful operation of the information system
    - Responsible for the implementation of information security controls as prescribed by the information security program and the data owner
    - Responsible for notifying the information security program and the data owner of any change that may change the information security risk of the information system
    - Ensure that audit and logging mechanisms exist and that they are reviewed and provided to the security operations center
    - Ensuring that an asset inventory is maintained for the information system and any of its subcomponents
    - Ensure that data sanitization procedures are followed in accordance with information security and data owner requirements when the information system is decommissioned
- **IT custodian**: IT custodians are IT personnel who provide information system support. IT custodians typically work for the system owner and are responsible for carrying out the requirements provided by the system owner, data owner, and information security program. Such responsibilities include, but are not limited to:
    - Executes operation and maintenance procedures on the information system
    - Ensures information security controls are implemented and working
    - Documents and executes changes to the information system
    - Reviews logs and executes audits for the information system
    - Executes sanitization and disposal procedures when the information system is decommissioned

Defining enforcement authority

The information security plan should establish the information security program as the group responsible for the establishment of information security policy and clearly define who is responsible for following that policy.

Enforcement areas:

- **People**: Define the types of users that will be bound by information security policies (staff, contractors, students, and so on)
- **Technology**: Define the enterprise technology scope under the authority of the information security program

Pulling it all together

Now that you have defined your information security program's strategy and initiatives, it is time to take the information learned throughout this book and begin to assemble your information security program, executing the necessary projects ensuring that you keep business needs at the forefront.

Summary

In this chapter, we learned about the concepts necessary to develop an enterprise information security program plan. Remember that this program plan is a foundational document that will be used to establish how your information security program will function and interact with the rest of the business.

In this chapter, you learned:

- How to develop your information security program objectives
- You discovered elements that will assist you in creating a successful information security program
- We discussed aligning your information security program with the business
- We worked through key concepts in the development of the information security program plan

In the next chapter, we will be discussing continuous testing and monitoring. We will discover the various types of testing we can utilize to ensure information security controls have been deployed properly, and we will discuss how to best implement testing across the life of an information system.

6
Continuous Testing and Monitoring

Vulnerabilities are part of the life cycle of the modern information system. Software and hardware are rushed to market with often inadequate testing, resulting in an organizational information system that is a patchwork of potentially highly vulnerable systems. It is important for the information security professional to understand that vulnerabilities in information systems are a fact of life that is not going away anytime soon. The key to protecting the modern information system is continued vigilance through continuous technical testing.

In this chapter, you will learn:

- Technical testing categories at your disposal
- Testing integration into the SDLC
- Continuous monitoring considerations
- Vulnerability assessment considerations
- Penetration testing considerations

Types of technical testing

- **Vulnerability assessment**: Vulnerability scanning serves to interrogate a specific information system or an entire network to discover weaknesses in their security posture.
- **Web application vulnerability assessment**: A specific type of vulnerability assessment that is targeted at web-based applications versus servers and networks. This type of assessment attempts to find weaknesses in application code and logic.
- **Static code analysis**: Static code analysis inspects the source code of an application and attempts to determine whether flaws exist that could be exploited by an attacker.
- **Penetration testing**: Penetration testing takes the results of vulnerability assessments and validates that an identified weakness is an exploitable vulnerability.

SDLC considerations for testing

Security testing fits into all parts of the SDLC/SELC and plays a vital role in ensuring the security of the information system, from project initiation until the information system has reached the end of its useful life and it is disposed of.

Project initiation

Conduct analysis of business needs: The information security professional must work closely with the business/mission users and the information technology staff to have a firm grasp of the solution that is required by the business and proposed by IT. This is an opportunity for the information security professional to add value to the project team by providing alternatives and ensuring that a secure proposal is developed.

During this phase, you will typically be conducting solution reviews versus outright technical testing. This is a very important part of the overall project life cycle, since this is where key project decisions are made from a business vision and technical direction perspective. These decisions will affect the information system throughout its entire life cycle, and it is imperative that the information security professional has a seat at the table.

Requirements analysis

- **Perform initial security risks assessment**: As the information security professional is working with your business and IT stakeholders, you should be able to gather enough information to build an initial security risk assessment that will allow you to better inform the project. This is an excellent time to perform data categorization, which was discussed in the risk management chapter.
- **Ensure that security requirements are testable**: It is important that you develop testable information security requirements as part of the overall project requirements for the information system. Simply put, if you develop a requirement that you cannot test, you have most likely developed a bad requirement. In the following example, the first requirement for logging is vague. If you implement logging but do not have the ability to log specific events, you will not be able to properly secure the information system. The second example is much better. In this example, we are giving specific testable elements that can be used to build the information system's logging capability:
    - **Bad requirement example**: The information system must implement logging
    - **Bad requirement example**: The information system must audit events related to the successful login and logout of privileged users

System design

- **Develop the test plan**: Now that you have testable requirements for the information system and you are in the design phase, it is time to develop the test plan, test procedures, and mechanisms you will use to report the results of the information security test that you perform. Your test plan should answer the following questions:
    - What is the scope of the test?
    - Who will be conducting the test?
    - What is required to conduct the test (tools, personnel, and so on)?
    - How should the outputs of the testing be handled (company proprietary, confidential, and so on)?
    - If a system outage or a security event occurs, who should be contacted?

Your test procedures should be carefully planned to include all the necessary steps to conduct the test, including the information needed to ascertain whether a test has passed or failed. In the following example, the tester is validating a web application for a cross-site scripting vulnerability. The tester enters the cross-site scripting exploit code `<script>alert(123)</script>` into an input field on the web application and submits the request to the web server. If the web browser returns an alert box that says `123`, the test has failed and the input field in the web application is vulnerable to cross-site scripting. Otherwise, the test has passed and the input field is not vulnerable. The tester would continue to test all input fields using this test to ensure each input field is not vulnerable to cross-site scripting:

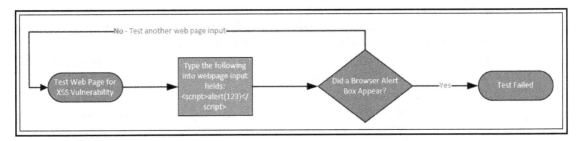

Finally, develop a reporting mechanism where you clearly provide the results of the security test for the project team. The report should include the identified vulnerabilities and recommended mitigation necessary to close the discovered vulnerabilities. The results of the testing should include both passed and failed tests, with artifacts supporting the tester's assertion. The report should be provided to the appropriate individual(s) in your organization, following the data handling guidance that was previously identified in the test plan.

- **Testing throughout the design process**: The information security professional will be engaged with the information system design team throughout the development process. While there is a clear part of the SDLC that is reserved for the acceptance testing of the information system, the information security professional will perform the required testing services throughout the design process to ensure that security services are working as expected and do not hinder the expected functioning of the information system.

It is very important that the information security professional be well-engaged in this part of the SDLC, as this is where the design elements are being tested and proof of concepts implemented in support of the future production information system. Being part of this process serves to ensure that security is part of the information system and that it has been designed in; not being part of this process runs the risk of security services not being adequately implemented, which will result in inadequate protections for the production information system.

System implementation

Testing updates and emergency changes: Things don't always go as planned and the information security professional should not expect that to change when it comes to implementing an information system. The information security professional should be available during the implementation phase of the system to assist with changes that were not anticipated during the design phase. Having the information security professional present ensures that security guidance can be provided for any required changes to the design of the information system, helping to ensure an acceptable level of security. Additionally, the information security professional can test the new changes to the design to validate that the security controls are functioning as expected and not impacting the system being implemented.

System testing

Execute the test plan: Now that the system has been fully implemented, this is where the information security professional performs the formal assessment of the information security controls that have been implemented for the information system. The testing that is included in this phase can utilize many tools and techniques to ascertain that the confidentiality, integrity, and availability of the information system is appropriately protected, commensurate with the value of the data contained within it.

The testing included in this phase will examine the operational, management, and technical control of the information system. From a technical perspective, the tester will be able to utilize security specific tools to conduct a vulnerability assessment and/or the penetration testing of the new production information system. From a management and operational perspective, the information security professional will conduct a security assessment to *interview, document, observe,* or *test* security controls that cannot be readily reviewed through automated means.

Once the test plan has been fully executed, the tester will return the results to the implementation team and management as appropriate. Any security controls that were not properly implemented or are missing will be implemented now. An iterative process will then be engaged to validate changes and test them. Once all tests have passed, or management has accepted the risk on failed tests, the testing phase will conclude.

Operations and maintenance

The operations and maintenance phase is the years between the implementation and disposition phases, where the information system is providing a useful service to the organization. Testing will be conducted on the information system periodically to ensure that the security of the information system is maintained. The two triggers that will cause the information system to be tested are:

- **Scheduled**: You will want to conduct a periodic vulnerability assessment and penetration testing on a scheduled basis, depending on your corporate policies.
- **Information system changes**: Any time that a new change occurs to the information system, you will want to conduct a test to ensure that the information security of the information system is still adequate:
    - **Example of a significant change**: A new version release of a software package or operating system

Disposition

Media sanitization: As part of the disposition process for an information system, the information security professional will work with the IT staff to ensure that all media devices have been fully sanitized and that sensitive organizational data is not inadvertently accessed due to eliminated information technology assets.

SDLC summary

The following diagram provides an example of the security testing responsibilities that the information security professional is responsible for in their organization. This diagram is still a very high-level representation of the potential testing possibilities that can occur throughout the SDLC of an information system.

It is important to note that you must ensure a very delicate balance between testing and improving security on one side, and encumbering your program teams and having them avoid you on the other.

Here are some best practices that I have encountered to ensure success throughout the SDLC regarding information security testing:

- When possible, work with your developer and IT teams to integrate security testing into their testing/quality assurance gates. Do not force other teams to adopt your arbitrary schedule.
- Do not pretend that you are the subject matter expert for everything! Work with your SME teams to establish workable solutions to address failed security tests.
- Provide lots of guidance around security requirements. Most teams want to build secure systems. Providing this guidance gives your developers and IT teams the tools they need to secure the information system.

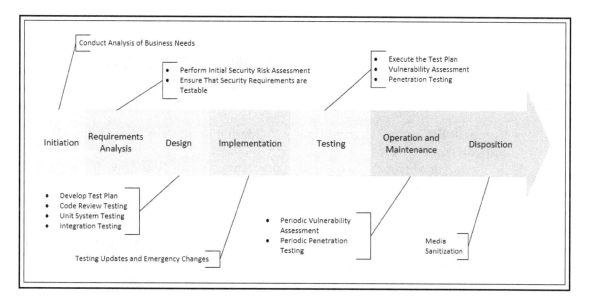

Continuous monitoring

The concept of continuous monitoring comes from the idea that an information system that is not checked often will begin to develop exploitable weaknesses. The IT and information security team can do an amazing job in developing, securing, and testing a new information system. However, this work is a point-in-time activity and becomes stale very rapidly. As new patches come out or new exploit techniques are developed, the information system must be updated to reflect these new threats.

Continuous monitoring lives in the operations and management phase of the system development life cycle. A well-developed continuous monitoring program should be established within your organization to ensure that security controls around people, processes, and technologies are effectively monitored and continue to be well defending against the ever-changing information security threat landscape. Key concepts to consider as you begin to plan and implement a continuous monitoring program in your organization are discussed in the following sections.

Information security assessment automation

These are tool that are implemented by the information security program to perform automated assessment of organizational standards related to:

- **Vulnerability and patch compliance**: Validating information system patch levels and vulnerability across the enterprise to include:
    - Server and workstation operating systems (Windows, Linux, and so on)
    - Network devices (Routers, Switches, and so on)
    - Server software applications (Database, email, DNS, and so on)
    - Desktop applications (Microsoft Word, Adobe Acrobat, and so on)
- **Network and configuration management**: Ensuring compliance with organizational change management policies as well as information security baselines:
    - Manages the thousands of configuration items related to the information system and allows for common secure configurations
    - Performs the discovery and inventory of information system assets
    - Discovery and restriction of unauthorized software and hardware

- **Software assurance**: The development and implementation of software that is free from exploitable vulnerabilities and works as intended:
    - Static code analysis
    - Web application vulnerability scanners
    - Database vulnerability scanners
- **License and asset management**: Tools that help the organization make an inventory of hardware and software locations on the enterprise network or individual information system:
    - These tools offer management of software deployment and provisioning, asset discovery and information collection, and software and hardware usage.
    - These functions may be integrated into other tools implemented by the organization. For example, your network or configuration management tools may include asset management.

Effective reporting of information security status

Reporting tools and dashboards allow you to have visibility into your overall security posture, which in turn allows you to understand the information security risk associated with an information system. Many of the tools that you implement as part of your information security program support this requirement and can be used in conjunction with an enterprise reporting tool, or can be used to feed an overall enterprise tool.

Governance risk and compliance: Tools that allow the information security program to:

- Distribute the information security policy to project teams
- Maintain mapping of the organizational information security policy against applicable compliance standards
- Test information system implementation of controls against the organizational information security policy
- Perform risk assessment and schedule mitigations
- Provide reporting of the organization's information security risk posture

Alerting of information security weakness

It includes tools that are designed to continuously poll the information system for changes that introduce an exploitable vulnerability:

- **Incident and event management**: Tools that are constantly inspecting enterprise systems and applications for indicators of compromise:
  - Intrusion detection systems
  - Security information and event management
  - Log management
- **Malware detection**: Tools that allow for the detection of *trojans, spyware, viruses,* and other malicious code throughout the enterprise information system. The best approach is to implement multiple layers of malware detection throughout your network:
  - **Server and workstation operating system**: Traditional antivirus installed on the operating system
  - **Gateway level protection**: Email message transfer agent, web proxy, and virtualized malware detonation appliances
- **Information management**: Tools that protect information within the organization at rest within organizational information systems and from unauthorized exfiltration by attackers. Data loss prevention tools serve to protect information from theft or misuse by internal employees or external attackers. These tools, when properly configured, not only protect the organization's information, but also alert the information security professional that a potential compromise has occurred.

Vulnerability assessment

Vulnerability assessment is a methodology used to determine whether an exploitable weakness exists on an information system. This is important to stress as vulnerability assessment is not a tool. While performing a vulnerability assessment, you will use many tools. While good tools are required for a successful vulnerability assessment, it is the skill of the tester and the adherence to process that ensures a high-quality vulnerability assessment.

Business relationship with vulnerability assessment

The vulnerability assessment that you perform will most likely find hundreds of vulnerabilities in your environment and could very easily find thousands. The modern information system, due to its complexity and the fact that software is not designed in a secure manner, will develop many vulnerabilities over time. Without an effective means of triaging the vulnerabilities that you discover, you may find it very difficult to effectively secure your organization. Understanding what is important to your business will help you to prioritize the protection of the information system in the order to reduce the risk in the most effective way for your business.

Vulnerability scanning

There are many methods that can be used to scan your network for existing vulnerabilities. Some of these mechanisms include:

- **Port scanning**: A type of scan that determines whether a computer has open TCP or UDP ports. If a port is open on a computer, it means that a network service is running and is listening on that port.
- **Network tracing**: A scan that attempts to build a network map based on the results returned by the scan.
- **Version scanning**: The version scan adds to the port scan by attempting to determine which service and what version of that service is running on a given port.
- **Network sweeping**: This type of scan is used to determine what IP addresses are in use by network connected devices.
- **OS fingerprinting**: Like version scanning in that the scanner attempts to guess the version of the operating system based on data returned by the scan.

Vulnerability scanning process

The vulnerability scanning process follows a basic workflow where the tester will initiate a series of scans. Each scan builds on the next, providing more information each time so that the tester builds an accurate understanding of the environment, which then leads to the actual vulnerability scan:

Device Discovery	Service Enumeration	Vulnerability Scanning	Vulnerability Validation

• Syn Scan
• Ping
	• Operating System
	  Services
	• UDP Ports
	• TCP Ports
		• Missing Patches
		• Unneeded Services
		• Configuration
		  Validation
			• Validate Findings
			• False Positive
			  Removal

This is the workflow to perform a successful vulnerability scan:

1. **Device discovery**: During this phase of the workflow, the tester maps out the devices that are present on the network. Additionally, the tester scans to determine the topology of the network where the devices being scanned reside:
   - **Scans performed**: Network tracing, port scanning, network sweeping

2. **Service enumeration**: During this phase of the workflow, the tester determines what services and what operating systems reside on the target machines being scanned. This information is vital to ensure an accurate vulnerability scan:
   - **Scan performed**: Version scanning, OS fingerprinting

If effective service enumeration is not accomplished, the tester may receive inaccurate results during the vulnerability scan. For instance, a vulnerability that exists on a specific open port for a Linux system may not exist on a Windows system. If the OS fingerprinting does not accurately fingerprint the operating system, your vulnerability scan may say that you have a vulnerability when you don't, because the vulnerability scanner thought it was scanning a different operating system.

The best way to perform these activities is through automation and the selection of great tools. There are many free and paid tools that can be used to perform these activities.

An excellent tool for performing device discovery and service enumeration on your network is a tool called **Nmap** (**Network Mapper**)—https://nmap.org/. The Nmap tool is open source software and is free to use. Nmap is an industry accepted tool and is very popular among security professionals. This means that there is an incredible amount of resources available to learn Nmap and if you get stuck, you will be able to easily find an answer to your question.

Nmap is a great tool and best yet it is free to use for personal and commercial use. Follow the link given here to learn how to use this amazing resource.

The reference guide on using the Nmap tool is located at: https://nmap.org/book/man.html.

3. **Vulnerability scanning**: The goal of vulnerability scanning is to determine whether exploitable weaknesses exist in the underlying information systems that you are scanning. You will take the results from your device discovery and service enumerations phases, and input them into your vulnerability scanning tool. The vulnerability scanner will use multiple methods in determining whether a specific muliebrity exists, including:

    - **Validating configuration**: The scanning tools examine the operating system and service configuration, validating that the configuration meets a given security standard.
        - **Organizational policies:** Your vulnerability scanner will typically come preloaded with some base set of security scans enabled so that you can check your information systems from a best practices perspective. This is great! However, what you need to do is ensure that your vulnerability scanner is configured to inspect your information systems against your organization's security policy.
        - **Unauthenticated scans**: In this case, a tester is performing a vulnerability scan with no administrative privileges. This means that you will not be able to see configurations from operating systems and services that require elevated permissions. Unauthenticated scans should be avoided if possible so that you can gather a more accurate picture of the vulnerabilities in the system.

Some will say that by performing an unauthenticated scan you are getting a better picture of what an attacker will see. This is true to a certain extent. However, if you are working with your internal teams to secure your enterprise environment, you should be working to close all exploitable vulnerabilities, not just the ones that you think an attacker might see.

- **Authenticated scans:** These are the preferred scans that you should choose to run against your information systems. The authenticated scan has the operating system-level permissions necessary to get deep into the configuration of the information system and properly test for any invalid configurations.

Running authenticated scans poses a higher risk to the information system then unauthenticated scans, since authenticated scans have the means to make changes to the information system; it has the permissions needed to do so. Most vulnerability scanning tools have options to run tests that are considered less safe or not safe. This means you are taking the risk of crashing an information system if you run those specific scans. You should only run these types of scans if you have approval from/have notified your information system owner and have taken appropriate measures to fully back up the information system.

- **Validating service behavior**: Validating service behavior can lead to the discovery of old and potentially vulnerable software residing on the information system. For example, if you find that port 22 is open through a port scan, and you determine that SSH is running on this port, your vulnerability scanner can interact with the service to see whether it responds like an older vulnerable version of SSH. If it does not, it may be a newer version. If it does behave like an older version, the service may be vulnerable to exploitation.
- **Validating version**: The version validation performed by the vulnerability scanner dives much deeper into the information system being tested than what was performed during service enumeration. The vulnerability scanner will inspect installed software packages on the information system for old versions, including those packages that do not listen on network ports.

- **Available vulnerability scanners**: There are currently many vulnerability scanners, and these range in effectiveness and cost. Here is a list of some available scanners:

Scanner	Free/paid	URL
GFI LanGuard	Paid	`https://www.gfi.com`
MBSA	Free	`https://www.microsoft.com`
Core Impact	Paid	`https://www.coresecurity.com`
Nessus	Paid	`https://www.tenable.com`
Nexpose	Paid	`https://www.rapid7.com`
QualysGuard	Paid	`https://www.qualys.com`
OpenVAS	Free	`http://www.openvas.org`
Retina	Paid	`https://www.beyondtrust.com`

4. **Vulnerability validation**: Once the vulnerability scanner has run through its operation, you will now need to work through the result. One of the most frustrating things you can do to your project team is to hand over a vulnerability assessment result report fresh out of your scanning tool, without doing validation to ensure that the report is accurate.

It is important to understand that the vulnerability scanner is scanning to find weaknesses based on a signature or rule in the tool's database. It is entirely possible, and happens often, that a vulnerability scanner will state that a vulnerability has been found when one does not exist. This is because a valid signature or rule in the vulnerability scanning tools found a match on the information system for software or configurations that match the signature or rule but are not vulnerable. Here are some examples:

- **Problem**: A Windows system is flagged as a Linux system. The vulnerability scanner then flags an open port as vulnerable based on the assumption that the system is Linux. However, the actual Windows system is not vulnerable.
  - **Resolution**: Flag the system as Windows and rescan

- **Problem**: The vulnerability scanner states that a patch is not installed on a Windows system. However, a rollup patch that contains the patch in question was installed. This means that the scanner did not analyze the rollup patch as having contained this patch.

  - **Resolution:** Enable the ability for your scanner to detect rollup patches and rescan

Vulnerability resolution

The vulnerability resolution process comes after the information security professional has completed their testing and has validated the findings in the vulnerability scanning report. The job of the information security professional is not over now that the report and metrics are being handed over to the operations and/or development teams for mitigation. The information security professional should work closely with these teams, providing the necessary support to explain uncovered vulnerabilities and to work with the teams to understand how the vulnerabilities where uncovered. The vulnerability resolution process workflow includes the following stages:

1. **Investigate vulnerabilities**: The operation and/or development team needs to dig deep into the information system and verify that the vulnerabilities identified in the vulnerability scan report do in fact exist. The technical teams responsible for the information system will work through the identified vulnerabilities to:
   - **Check whether vulnerabilities identified are valid**: While the information security professional has validated the vulnerabilities, the subject matter experts responsible for the information system will still need to ensure that the vulnerabilities are valid.
     - If a vulnerability is deemed invalid, the information security professional should work with the technical team to validate that there is, in fact, no vulnerability and note this in the vulnerability assessment report.
   - **Determine a plan of action**: The technical team, working with the information security professional, will develop the steps necessary to mitigate the vulnerability. These steps could include mitigation activities such as:
     - The installation of a patch
     - The upgrading of an operating system
     - The closing of a network port
     - The changing of a server or service configuration

2. **Resolve vulnerability**: It is now time to close the vulnerability. The technical team for the information system deploys the plan of action to mitigate the discovered vulnerability.

3. **Report status**: The technical team after having implemented the plan of action to resolve the vulnerability reports the status as successful or unsuccessful back to the information security team:

    - If the vulnerability was not successfully resolved, the information security professional will should work with the technical team to resolve the issue and develop a new plan as necessary.

4. **Retest the information system**: Once the vulnerability has been satisfactorily resolved, the information security professional will retest the information system to ensure that the vulnerability has been resolved. If the vulnerability has been resolved, it will be noted in the vulnerability assessment report and closed. If the vulnerability was not resolved, this process will begin again with the technical team:

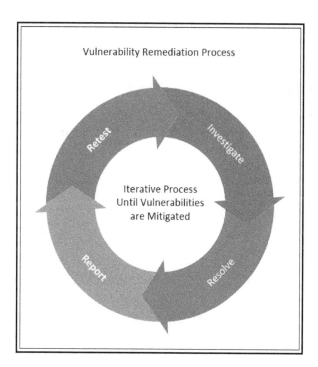

Penetration testing

Penetration testing is a planned attack on an information system that attempts to simulate what an actual information system would experience if it was being attacked by a hacker. The types of penetration tests that the organization can choose to implement include:

- **Social engineering**: This type of test attempts to lure a user into revealing information that would benefit an attacker in further exploiting the organization. Information that the attacker would look to gain from a user includes:
  - **Client-side**: This type of test serves to test the end user environment by testing applications on the desktop environment.
  - **Wireless security**: This test attempts to discover and exploit and organization's wireless networking capability.
  - **Network services**: This type of test looks to exploit systems and services located on the enterprise network.
  - **Physical security**: This type of test looks to exploit the physical security of the organization, such as locks and alarms.

Phases of a penetration test

The penetration testing process is a highly choreographed and repeatable process that provides you with the assurance that you are conducting the necessary activities to perform a quality test.

1. **Reconnaissance**: In the reconnaissance phase, the penetration tester seeks to gather information about the organization that will allow them to exploit and penetrate the organization's defenses. Types of reconnaissance include:
   - **Active**: The tester actively gathers data about the organization. An example of active reconnaissance is port scanning, where you are directly interacting with the system that you intend to exploit.
   - **Passive**: The tester passively gathers data about the organization and does not directly interact with the information system that they intend to exploit. Examples include dumpster diving and phishing emails.

2. **Scanning**: In this phase of the attack, the tester seeks to gain additional information about the network that they are attempting to infiltrate. A tester would perform an activity such as a vulnerability scan in this phase of the test.

3. **Gaining access**: In this phase of the test, the tester seeks to gain control of the information system that they are testing. Now that the tester has uncovered vulnerabilities, after having completed the scanning phase, the tester seeks to exploit those vulnerabilities to gain access. During this phase, the tester will also attempt to get deeper into the network by using their initially exploited machine to begin attacking other devices on the network. Remember that any device that is on your network has the potential to be exploited. It is easier to think of workstations and servers being vulnerable to attack. However, your networking gear (routers, switch, firewalls, and so on), if not properly maintained, can easily open you up to attack.

What may be harder to realize is that with the proliferation of the **Internet of Things (IoT)**, your organization's thermostats may provide an excellent source for exploitation. As the information security professional, you must be ready to test all the devices on your network and be ready to secure and defend those devices.

4. **Maintaining access**: Once the tester has acquired access to your network, the next thing they will do is ensure that they keep access. The tester will install software that will allow them to access the compromised device even if the vulnerability that allowed the compromise to be exploited is closed. Tools that can be used to maintain access include:
    - **Backdoors**: Tools running in the background on the affected system that allows the tester to access the system remotely and without detection.
    - **Malware (Viruses, trojans, worms, botnets, and so on)**: These tools are used for exploitation and data exfiltration. If properly crafted, they can be used to maintain access in a pen test or attack scenario.
    - **Purpose-built software packages**: Tools such as Core Impact and Metasploit allow the tester to maintain access of a compromised system.

5. **Covering tracks**: You will want to ensure that you are covering your tracks as part of a successful penetration test, since this is what an attacker would do. A skilled attacker would not set off your security operations center alarms. Therefore, it is important that you take the same great care to cover your tracks as part of the pen test so that the scenario is like an actual attack. An example of covering your tracks at the network level would be to use a:

- **Reverse HTTPS shell**: In this scenario, the tester has installed a piece of software on the compromised machine that caused the machine to reach out to the tester's command and control device at regular intervals. To an internal monitoring team, this looks like regular secured web traffic when in fact it is a compromised system looking for commands from the tester/attacker.

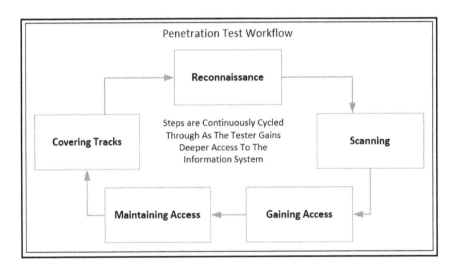

Difference between vulnerability assessment and penetration testing

As you can see, there is a significant difference between a vulnerability assessment and a penetration test. The vulnerability assessment's primary purpose is to determine whether vulnerabilities exist on the target device being assessed, while the penetration test is concerned with understanding whether those vulnerabilities can be used to gain access to that system and in turn gain access to sensitive organizational information.

The difference of the two types of test is clearly observed by reviewing their workflows. The vulnerability assessment ends at the scanning phase of the penetration test. Where you would begin to work with your technical team to remedy vulnerabilities in the vulnerability assessment, the penetration tester continues testing to compromise the target system, resulting in control of that system.

A penetration test is also about being able to show that information security vulnerabilities present in the underlying information system can result in the exfiltration of sensitive data. A key activity in penetration testing is being able to show that the tester can not only gain access to an information system, but also use that access to gain deeper access to the enterprise network and gain access to sensitive information. A vulnerability assessment does not attempt to provide this level of information security visibility.

Examples of successful attacks in the news

The reason that we perform so much testing is to ensure that the organization's information systems are protected from attack. Here are some examples of publicized attacks. These attacks could have been prevented if their organizations had tested and mitigated these vulnerabilities. If this had occurred, the attacker would not have had a vulnerability to exploit.

Point of sale system attacks

The **point of sale** (POS) systems are cash registers. You may be thinking what is the big deal about cash registers and how can people break into my network by attacking a cash register? The reality is that modern POS systems are typically fully functioning operating systems that expose services that can be exploited by an attacker.

Vendor	Date reported	Settlement amount	URLs
Target	December 19, 2013	$18.5 million	http://www.latimes.com/business/la-fi-target-credit-settlement-20170523-story.html
Home Depot	September 8, 2014	$19.5 million	https://threatpost.com/home-depot-agrees-to-19-5-million-settlement-to-end-2014-breach-nightmare/116884/

Cloud-based misconfigurations

In these attacks, companies allowed data to be exposed on cloud-based servers that they did not configure properly, leading to the exposure of sensitive data. It is incredibly important to remember that your organization is responsible for the configuration of your cloud services. Shifting your technology to a third party does not remove your responsibility regarding data protection.

Vendor	Date reported	Data disclosed	URLs
Booz Allen Hamilton	May 13, 2017	Sensitive US Federal Government Information	`https://www.cyberscoop.com/ booz-allen-hamilton-amazon- s3-chris-vickery/`
Viacom	September 19, 2017	Internal company IT configurations	`https://www.theregister.co. uk/2017/09/19/viacom_ exposure_in_aws3_bucket_ blunder/`
Verizon Wireless	September 22, 2017	Internal Company IT Configurations	`https://www.theregister.co. uk/2017/09/22/verizon_falls_ for_the_old_unguarded_aws_s3_ bucket_trick_exposes_ internal_system/`

Summary

The introduction of vulnerabilities into the information system is clearly part of the life cycle of the modern information system. Organizations rush information systems into production without adequate testing, resulting in potentially highly vulnerable systems. The key to protecting your organization's information system is continued vigilance through continuous technical testing.

In this chapter, we learned:

- The categories of technical testing and how to take advantage of them
- How to integrate the various categories of information security testing into the SDLC
- Considerations related to vulnerability assessment, penetration testing, and continuous monitoring

In the next chapter, we will learn about **business continuity and disaster recovery (BCDR)** planning. We will discuss the many considerations around how to implement a successful BCDR plan, leading to continued business operations in the event of a disaster.

7

Business Continuity/Disaster Recovery Planning

Business continuity and disaster recovery planning encompass two separate but related disciplines that work together to:

- **Business continuity planning**: Ensure that an organization can effectively understand what business processes and information are important to the continued operations and success of the organization
- **Disaster recovery planning**: How to develop a technical solution that supports the business needs of the organization in the event of a system outage

In this chapter, you will learn:

- The scope and focus areas of the BCDR plan
- Designing, implementing, testing, and maintaining the BCDR plan

Scope of BCDR plan

BCDR is the combination of two interrelated business concepts. In this section, we will explore the concepts of *business continuity* and *disaster recovery*.

Business continuity planning

A business continuity plan looks at the risks and threats that face an organization and establishes a mechanism to ensure that business functions can continue to operate in the event of a disaster.

The key input for the information security professional when it comes to business continuity planning is from business or mission stakeholders. The key term in business continuity planning is business. The focus should not initially be on technology as technology serves to enable the business to do its work. Rather, the focus should be on the business functions that technology is supporting.

Key questions that you should be answering as you are developing your business continuity plan include:

- **What are your organizational risks**: As part of your information security program, you should be well versed in discussing risks with your organization. In fact, you may have already had this discussion with your organization, and business continuity may be the conversation that has naturally flowed out of your risk management program. If you haven't begun discussing organizational risks, now is the time as you can't begin developing a business continuity plan without understanding the negative impacts your organization can suffer. Questions you can ask include:
  - Are there geographical risks that can affect the operations of our organizations (hurricanes, wildfires, floods, blizzards)?
  - What will be the impact of a major disruption? What will the consequences be to the organization from a revenue and reputation perspective?
  - How will the organization continue to earn revenue in the event of a disaster (e-commerce website redundancy, manufacturing plant control systems)?
    - What products and services does your organization provide and how will you continue to provide these products and services in the event of a disaster?

- **How does your organization's location affect its availability**: Determine if your organization would be unable to continue operating if key locations became unavailable.

For example, does your organization rely too heavily on a headquarters? If the building became unavailable, would the organization cease to function? If you could answer yes to that question, you have a problem. Organizations take different approaches to solve this issue, including the following:

- The establishment of satellite locations that will take over key capabilities in the event of a disaster. These locations are typically part of the organization. Key team members would move to these locations and continue their roles from these satellite locations.
- Developing a plan to establish an emergency command center at a predefined location. In this case, an alternate location such as a hotel may be defined where team members will move to re-establish operations.
- The organization may move to a full telework capability until operations can be reinstated in the primary work facility.

- **Do you have a succession plan**: What will you do if a key member of your team is unavailable? We tend to be morbid when we think about this, but let's be positive. What will you do when one of your key team members gets hit by the lottery? They are alive and well but will not be supporting your organization anymore. Also, you can have a situation where a key team member is available to work but environmental conditions have cut the team member off from the organization. You must have the necessary plans in place to ensure that you have the human resources available to continue operating your organization. Questions to ask include:
  - Who takes key executive leadership roles over if top-level positions members are unavailable or incapacitated?
  - Are technical details properly documented so that if key technical resources are not available, business continuity actions can still be taken?
  - Do you have team members cross-trained in duties so that you can perform at least minimal functionality (hopefully more) in the event of a disaster?
    - How will you continue to pay your staff?

Disaster recovery planning

A disaster recovery plan is a documented set of steps whereby an organization establishes the process and procedures necessary to recover an information system in the event of a disaster.

A disaster recovery plan takes the concerns and requirements of your organization's business/mission that the leaders developed during business continuity planning and translates it into actionable steps that will allow your organization to continue operating in the event of a disaster. Questions that you should be asking as part of the disaster recovery planning process include:

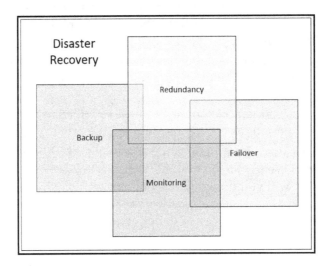

- **Where is the money coming from**: Resources are the key to an effective disaster recovery plan. Disaster recovery will cost your organization money. This cost should be commensurate with the risk appetite of senior leadership and the value of the information that will continue to be available in the event of a disaster:
    - **Expected expenses**: As part of the planning process, you will derive concrete expectations regarding what it will take to establish alternate operations for your organization. These will be approved funds or part of the expected organizational budget to ensure business continuity.
    - **Unexpected expense**: A plan is only good the moment it is completed. After that, unexpected scenarios will be introduced causing your plans to change. What has your organization planned for addressing unplanned resource requirements during a disaster to ensure continued business continuity?

- **What are your disaster recovery team's roles**: The worst thing you can do from a disaster recovery perspective is to run around screaming and shouting. The point of all this planning is to establish the plans agreed to by all levels of management regarding what the organization will do in the event of a disaster:
    - **Who will lead the disaster recovery effort**: There should be an organizational leader and a leader within each business unit.
    - **Are roles clearly defined**: Who reports to whom? Who declares an emergency?
    - **Do individuals know how to contact each other**: Do you have a call tree? Is there a cadence for business units to communicate with each other for the purposes of status and information decimation?
- **Where is your data**: If your data is in a closet in your headquarters and your headquarters burn down, you have a problem. As part of the risk management and business continuity processes, you should have determined what information is highly critical to your organization and determined mechanisms to ensure that information is accessible and not located in a single, highly vulnerable location:
    - **Do you have failover site capability**: Do you have additional IT capability outside of a single geographically similar primary location where you can take over information processing capabilities?
    - **Is your data in the cloud**: Do you not have a data processing facility and have you moved your processing to a cloud provider? Ensure that you look at your contracts and ensure that you have the fault tolerance that you think that you have. The key takeaway is that not all cloud providers are made equal and your disaster recovery capability is your responsibility, not the cloud providers.
- **Does the disaster recovery plan introduce vulnerabilities**: It is important that we plan for success versus something mediocre. You should not develop a plan that ultimately will introduce vulnerabilities into your organization:
    - **Are your data backups introducing inconsistencies**: If the organization has determined something is critical, the information system should work flawlessly from a backup perspective.

- **Does your plan introduce opportunities for data exfiltration**: Remember, we are planning and not running around screaming and shouting in a panic. At no point should architectural decisions be made that will jeopardize the information security protections that have been established and supported by senior leadership. The disaster recovery plan that supports the continued operations of the business should leave it in the same secure state that it was in prior to an emergency.

  Resist the notion that vulnerability introduction is acceptable as you will only be operating the disaster recovery plan for a short time until normal operations are restored. You do not know how long your organization will be operating in an emergency status, and as a result should establish a plan that ensures the security of the organization is maintained.

- **How is the plan tested**: The key to total chaos being avoided in the event of a disaster is testing. If you have developed a disaster recovery plan and have never tested it, you run the risk of not using it at all and falling to an ad hoc procedure that can expose your organization to a crippling lack of business continuity and can also introduce information security vulnerabilities that could have been otherwise avoided.

The following diagram shows the continuous nature of business continuity and disaster recovery planning, and that if your organization is conducting this process effectively it will always be in some part of the cycle. This does not by any means require that your organization be overburdened by the process. However, it does mean that time be given to ensure that those items that are critical to the business are addressed:

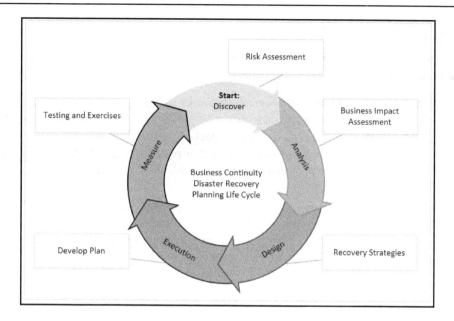

A key to success regarding business continuity and disaster recovery planning is to ensure that you are business-focused and not IT-focused. If the information security professional has done their job and ensured that the focus has been on critical business functions, your organization's leadership should be on board and willing to support the activity.

Additionally, since this activity starts off with business continuity and not IT continuity, you should ensure that you are picking your project sponsor and marketing this activity accordingly. As with most things that I have discussed in this book, the key is to enable the business and not perform information technology work for its own sake. This process should be championed and sponsored by an executive business leader in your organization with the information technology team supporting the goal of ensuring that the business will still be able to operate in the event of a disaster.

Focus areas for BCDR planning

Now that you have a handle on the basics of what business continuity and disaster recovery planning entail, it is now time to discuss in more detail the focus areas related to developing an effective plan.

We can break down the focus areas of BCDR planning into the categories of management, operational, and technical controls, which when combined provide a holistic approach to ensuring that business continuity is ensured.

Management

We look into policies, practices, and procedures at the organizational, information system, and personnel level:

- **Risk management**: BCDR specifically seeks to manage the risk associated with the outage of critical business services. It is however recommended that the BCDR risk management activities be part of a more holistic risk management program that is part of a mature information security program. In this way, the information security program can address BCDR concerns throughout the risk management life cycle.
- **Policies and strategies**: Policies and strategies are the outputs that you will develop that will help you ensure that your business can continue to function in the event of a disaster. These policies and strategies should address how the organization will respond to a disaster.

Operational

Security controls are implemented on an ongoing basis by individuals within the organization. Many of these control types deal with the day-to-day operations of the organizational information systems:

- **Organizational business continuity**: As an operational capability clearly defining your organization's business continuity objectives will serve feed lower level business unit and information system business continuity plans.
- **Individual business continuity plans**: Each business unit should develop specific business continuity plans, ensuring that they are in alignment with overall organizational plans and that there is a clear understanding regarding what is needed to keep individual business units operating in the event of a disaster.
- **Policies and procedures**: These policies and procedures are the detailed plans associated with disaster recovery. This is where the organization's business and IT units come together to build the steps to keep the organization operating during a disaster.

Technical

Security controls implemented on the information system that serves to protect the information system from unauthorized access are controls that are installed and reside on the information system by the IT team.

This part of BCDR is the actual technical implementations that are implemented before a disaster occurs that ensure a smooth transition during an emergency.

Depending on the organization's risk appetite and requirements developed during the business continuity discussions, the organization may choose to have a fully functioning mirror of the current operating environment, a reduced capability providing the minimum services necessary to get through a disaster, or a hybrid somewhere in between. To achieve these goals, the information technology group will implement services including:

- **Offsite replication**: Offsite replication ensures that key information services exist in real time at multiple data centers or cloud instances. If one instance of a site is disrupted, another instance can be used in its place to continue business operations.
- **Data backups**: Data backups are implemented to ensure that a system can be effectively restored. The number of backups will vary based on the organization's policies.
- **Infrastructure**: Infrastructure (network, systems, and storage) is all the architecture that goes into the effective planning, design, and implementation of an effective disaster recovery plan.

The following figure highlights the fact that the business continuity and disaster recovery processes are truly complementary processes that flow into each other, ultimately leading to a well-developed process to ensure that the business has the people, processes, and technology necessary to recover from a disaster and maintain business continuity:

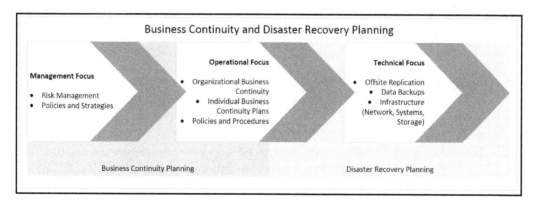

Designing the BCDR plan

The BCDR plan is an essential part of your organization's risk management strategy. This is where we take the information learned from the earlier part of this chapter and put it into practice.

As part of designing our BCDR plan, we will:

- Gather business requirements through the use of a BIA
- Define technical disaster recovery mechanisms
- Develop plan components that include:
    - Establishment of recovery teams
    - Establishment of relocation plans
    - Development of technical procedures to support recovery
    - BCDR testing and continuous improvement mechanisms

Requirements and context gathering – business impact assessment

The **business impact assessment (BIA)** is a key component of the overall business continuity process. With the business impact assessment, you are seeking to gather all the necessary information to allow the business to make the appropriate resource decisions that will allow for the effective creation of appropriate business continuity and disaster recovery plans.

Inputs to the BIA

The inputs to the BIA are coming from your business and mission team members. These inputs are used to inform the business continuity and disaster recovery process:

- **Business process supported**: You must clearly identify the business process that is supported when developing your BIA. This information will be looked at when developing the rationale behind why your organization should expend resources to operate this system during a disaster.
- **Information and services criticality**: This is where you define the specific data and information systems that support the business process identified previously.

- **Business impact**: Have the business think about and document what impact would occur to the business if the information or information systems identified in the BIA were to become unavailable.
- **Information systems utilized**: This is where you specifically identify what information systems are used to support the information used as part of the critical business process.
- **Allowable outage**: Have the business think about how long can they go without the information and/or the information system. This value is highly dependent on the type of information being discussed and the business unit in question, and therefore could vary wildly from group to group.

For example, the allowable outage for the organization's payroll system may be very different than an e-commerce application. The organization may decide that due to payroll processing requirements, an outage of 24 hours may be acceptable. However, the e-commerce application may only be able to endure an outage of a few minutes before the impact is considered too high.

- **Recovery priority**: This is where the business unit establishes how they want their information and information systems to be managed from a BCDR perspective from the information technology perspective.

This is typically accomplished by establishing a tiering system where the higher the tier number the lower the priority.

For example:

- The e-commerce application mentioned previously may be assigned as a tier one application where it is given a high priority to be recovered and has high resources given to ensure effective recovery.
- The payroll system may be defined as a tier two application. It has fewer resources assigned to its recovery since it has a greater allowable outage window.

This assignment of recovery priority is important for many reasons:

- It tells the IT team clearly how the business views criticality of the information system and what their expectations are from a recovery perspective.

- It ensures that the business understands the impact regarding resources and cost. A tier one application is usually very expensive to build a disaster recovery solution for.

If it is a business requirement, then it is money well spent. However, if it truly isn't business critical and therefore not tier one, its tier level can be reduced, saving the organization resources and money.

Outputs from the BIA

Outputs from the BIA are used to develop the disaster recovery strategy. This information will help the business to develop their business continuity plans and will assist the IT teams in developing their disaster recovery policy:

- **Recovery point objective**: The recovery point objective is the time that the IT team must be able to restore data from the past after an event has occurred. This is best understood as the time between the most recent backup and a disruption.
- **Recovery time objective**: The recovery time objective is the time that the IT team has to restore past data after an event has occurred.
- **Enterprise prioritization**: The IT team may have multiple applications living at the various prioritization tiers. This is where the IT and business teams discuss where an individual application will fall within the restoration priority.
- **Service level agreements**: Service level agreements are established so that clear expectations are developed between the business and IT teams.

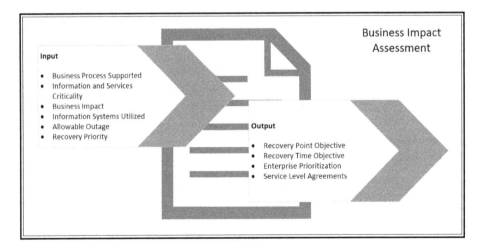

The BIA is a very useful document that serves to provide a clear set of requirements from the business and deliverables from the IT team. By going through the BIA process, both parties have a clear understanding of the business criticality associated with the data and how quickly information can be restored in the event of a failure.

Sample BIA form

The following is a sample BIA form that can be used to catalog business processes and information related to information systems and the data contained within them. The BIA process does not need to be overburdened with bureaucracy. One of the goals of the following form is to show you that you do not need to overcomplicate this process. The key pieces of information that you need to capture to ascertain business continuity and disaster recovery requirements are as follows:

Date:				Organization			
Point of Contact:				System Name			
System Owner:							
System Description:							
System Points of Contact				**Role**			
Business Process	**Impact**	**Allowable Outage**	**Recovery Priority**	**Software**	**Hardware**	**Dependencies / Interfaces**	

Define technical disasters recovery mechanisms

Now that you have developed clear requirements from your business stakeholders, it is time to begin developing the strategy that you will implement to technically reconstitute data and information systems if there were to be affected by an outage or a disaster.

Identify and document required resources

This is the point of the process where you begin to look at what your available options are based on your business user requirements and what you technically have at your disposal to properly meet your business continuity and disaster recovery requirements:

- Based on your business user requirements, what do you need?
- Develop a technical design that satisfies your business users' requirements.
- Ensure that information security is maintained as part of this design and that the organization's risk posture is not reduced by the design.

Conduct a gap analysis

Now that you have developed a design for your disaster recovery approach, it is time to perform a gap analysis against what you have designed and what is already in place.

If you designed a backup and recovery strategy that can be accomplished with already existing enterprise tools, then you do not have to add new capabilities to your network.

However, if your disaster recovery design includes a new data center including replication of data and information systems and that does not currently exist, that would be a gap.

Develop disaster recovery mechanisms

Now that you have a design and have conducted a gap analysis, it is time to develop your final approach and get approval from management. In this stage of defining your disaster recovery mechanism, you will explore what your various disaster recovery options will be. It makes sense at this stage to have sever plans to accomplish disaster recovery, as it is your business that is ultimately paying the bill.

Everyone wants an application to always be available until they receive a bill. Once reality sets in, many times the business may choose a less available disaster recovery option.

Once you have an approach that is acceptable to both IT and the business, it is time to develop the final architecture and develop the technical plan around any implementation strategies that may be required.

Develop your plan

Without a well thought out and coordinated plan with all key stakeholders, restoration of critical business functionality will be difficult or may fail completely.

Your plan framework will cover:

- Business-critical operation
- Business-critical assets
- Disaster recovery processes and procedures
- Assigned roles and responsibilities
- Communication procedures

Develop recovery teams

Develop a communication plan ensuring that you assign clear roles and responsibilities to individuals. Establishing these roles will help to ensure that in the event of disaster everyone has a clear script and set of duties to perform. Performing this activity will take the burden away from a communications perspective, making the recovery process operate more smoothly.

Establish relocation plans

This is the part of your disaster recovery plan where you establish how your organization will operate and where your IT will be serviced from:

- Will employees work from a new business location or will they telework?
- Will IT operate out of an alternate data center or will we utilize a cloud service?

During this stage, you need to ensure that you have covered all requirements, which include:

- **Storage requirements**:
    - Do you have enough storage to bring up new services?
- **Network connectivity**:
    - Can your users access the disaster recovery IT site?
    - Does the new site have the appropriate bandwidth?
    - Using the example of an e-commerce site, how will the rest of the world access the alternate site?

- **Licensing**:
    - How will the alternate processing facility's software be licensed?
    - Do you pay for the use of the site and its technology while it is not being used?
        - In traditional data centers, you typically would pay for unused resources
        - A cloud-based disaster recovery implementation may provide the ability to establish a plan without paying for resources until they are used

Develop detailed recovery procedures

IT systems are very complex. Attempting to stand up an alternate processing facility in support of business continuity is not a simple undertaking. Highly detailed, step-by-step plans must be developed to ensure that nothing is missed during a recovery operation. Most information systems must be restored in a very specific order with services that must be installed and started before other service will even work. A detailed plan will help you to implement services in the correct order, saving you troubleshooting time you will not be able to afford.

Test the BCDR plan

Testing is an important part of BCDR planning as it validates the effectiveness of the plan and establishes confidence that the business can continue to operate in the event of a disaster. Benefits of testing your BCDR plan include:

- Ensures that policies and procedures are understood by key roles and stakeholders
- Ensures that everyone knows what their communication responsibilities are in the event of a disaster
- Ensures that necessary equipment, technical tools, and facilities are available
- Ensures that individuals understand their roles and specific responsibilities in the event of a disaster
- Ensures that any gaps or weaknesses in the plan become evident so that the plan can be updated with the correct people, process, or technology to address the weakness

The purpose of testing is to ensure that the plan works as expected and that your organization and team members are up to the challenge of implementing the plan. If you discover that your plan is missing a component or that an approach doesn't work, it is time to update the plan.

Go back to the drawing board for that part of the plan and run back through the process, looking at your procedures to define where the ineffective component of the plan resides:

- Did you forget a clear communication step?
- Did you try to bring up an IT service out of order?
- Is there something wrong with your alternate facility or cloud service?

When you discover the ineffective plan component, replace it and retest. Continue this until you can fail over to disaster recovery operations and fail back to normal operations. Once you have accomplished this, you will have effectively tested your BCDR plan and can provide assurance to your business that operations can be maintained in the event of a disaster. The BCDR plan should be periodically tested to ensure that it is still effective technically and that current and new team members understand how to execute the plan.

Summary

In this chapter, we have learned the concepts of business continuity and disaster recovery planning that encompass two separate but related disciplines:

- **Business continuity planning**: Ensures that organizations effectively understand what business processes and information are important to them and what is required to ensure continued operations and success of the organization
- **Disaster recovery planning**: Develop the technical solutions that support the business needs of the organization in the event of a system outage

We also learned:

- What the scope and focus areas are of the BCDR plan
- How to design, implement, test, and maintain a BCDR plan

In the next chapter, we will be discussing the concepts around incident response planning and how your organization should prepare for detecting and responding to an intrusion attempt by an attacker.

8

Incident Response Planning

An incident response plan contains the plans and procedures implemented by your information security program. It ensures that you have adequate and repeatable processes in place to respond to any information security incident that could affect your organizational network or information systems.

This is very apparent from the following news stories:

- Pizza Hut PCI data breach:
    - First reported on October 14, 2017
    - For more information: `https://www.bleepingcomputer.com/news/security/users-report-fraudulent-transactions-after-pizza-hut-admits-card-breach/`
- Deloitte data breach affecting customers across governments and businesses:
    - First reported on September 25, 2017
    - For more information: `https://www.theguardian.com/business/2017/sep/25/deloitte-hit-by-cyber-attack-revealing-clients-secret-emails`

In this chapter, you will learn:

- Why you need an incident response plan
- What components make up the incident response plan
- Tools and techniques related to incident response
- The incident response process
- The OODA loop

Do I need an incident response plan?

Yes, you do. Information security breaches are inevitable in today's highly complex and extremely interconnected world. A well-thought-out incident response plan will help to ensure that you have all of the necessary processes and procedures to hunt for threats in your environment, ensure that those threats are properly contained and eradicated, and that you are able to properly restore your organization to a state where business can resume.

Regardless of the size of your organization, you need to ensure that you have a well-thought-out process for how your organization will respond in the event of an information security incident. Of course, the size and complexity of your incident response plan will vary greatly depending on the size and complexity of your organization. Additionally, an incident response plan is not weighed by the pound. Your incident response plan should be concise and to the point.

The incident response plan is key to the success of a well-functioning information security program. The incident response plan ensures that the information security program, IT organization, and business stakeholders have repeatable and agreed upon processes for the following:

- Containing
- Eradicating
- Recovering

These help guard against threats that actively engage your organization.

Components of an incident response plan

As with most concepts presented in this book, ultimately, the incident response plan is a business plan and must be designed and implemented with your organization's mission and business in mind. Essentially, the purpose of your incident response plan is to ensure that your organization can continue operating and providing services.

The incident response plan comprises many phases, which make up the overall incident response program life cycle. This life cycle includes:

- Initial activities that initiate, plan, and implement the incident response capability, including:
    - Ongoing dialog with the organization's IT and business stakeholders to ensure that the incident response capability meets business objectives

- The necessary planning to establish the organization's incident response capability as a functioning business program
- Establishment of a repeated life cycle that will characterize the incident response process for the organization
  - The repeatable operational processes involved in enterprise incident response:
    - These are the specific tactical procedures executed during an incident to mitigate the threat
  - Processes to gather lessons learned from a programmatic and operational perspective to update and improve the overall incident response capability:
    - Continuous process improvement should be a key component of your information security program including your incident response capability. As you are operating your incident response capability you will surely find places for improvement and areas where previously useful activities are no longer needed. Always be willing to take another look at your plans and adjust, ensuring that you are operating as efficiently and effectively as possible.

An important aspect of the incident response plan to remember is that your incident response activities should be focused on minimizing the impact to your organization where possible. Your incident response activities should be focused on ensuring that the threat is fully mitigated and operations can fully resume. You should not affect any other activities if you can avoid it.

Preparing the incident response plan

This includes not only the requirements needed to establish an enterprise incident response capability but also the necessary IT/cyber hygiene to ensure that enterprise and business unit information systems are properly defended.

The incident response program should not be siloed off from the rest of IT and information security planning. Considering this as the information responses capability is being planned any necessary technical updates that are discovered and are required to ensure that an information system is defensible should be captured and appropriately mitigated as part of the organization's risk management program.

Understanding what is important

As part of your preparation activities to conduct a successful incident response, you need to have a thorough understanding of what is important to your business/mission organization. If you have been following the guidance in this book to establish a successful information security program, then you have already worked with your stakeholders to determine key information, such as the following:

- Sensitive organizational data
- Sensitive information technology assets
- Your organization's risk appetite
- Allowable business process disruption
- How information systems are interconnected and communicating

If you haven't conducted these activities, then now is the time to engage your business and IT stakeholders and begin the process of understanding these key concepts. Begin peeling back the layers of complexity that is your organization and endeavor to understand concepts, such as the following:

- How your business applications and databases interact with each other
- How different business applications share information
- How servers that support these business applications are configured
- How the network is configured to ensure effective communications with business applications

Prioritizing the incident response plan

As you work to understand these concepts, ensure that you work closely with your business/mission stakeholders as this will provide you with context, allow you to prioritize what is important to the business, and allow you to respond accordingly. Based on business input, develop your list of the following:

- **Business applications/databases**: These are the applications that your business needs to function properly. A disruption in confidentiality, integrity, and availability will seriously disrupt the organization's ability to function.

- **Critical users**: Develop a list of users that are key to the successful operation of the organization. These users will typically cause a high negative impact on the organization if a threat actor causes them to perform an act against the organization:
  - VIPs—C-Suite and board-level employees
  - Key business users—individuals that have access to key organizational proprietary data and can cause that information to be released (comptroller and HR director)
  - IT administrators
- **Critical network and system services**: These are all the pieces of the enterprise network environment that are needed to provide the availability requirements for business data and applications.

Determining what normal looks Like

To determine if you have a threat actively exploiting your network you must first understand what your network normally looks like. Utilize tools such as those outlined later in this chapter to develop an automated view into the behavior of your network and your user population. By doing this, you will be able to understand if abnormal activity occurs, allowing your incident response identification phase to begin.

Observe, orient, decide, and act – OODA

A valuable concept that you can use to help conceptualize your incident response planning as well as your operational incident response capability is the OODA loop. The concept was originally developed by military strategist John Boyd and serves as a foundation when considering how to deal with an adversary, which is what the information security professional is doing as they are developing an incident response capability:

- **Observe**: Ensure that while you are planning your incident response capability that you have as much visibility into your information system as possible. The best defense that you can mount against modern well-funded and highly motivated adversaries is to implement advanced layer monitoring technologies. Your goal is to have in-depth visibility into your information systems' normal operations so that you can catch abnormal behavior.
- **Orient**: Here, you take the immense amount of information that you are gathering as part of your layered monitoring capability and apply additional tools and techniques to make better sense of the information, allowing you to triage and prioritize your actions.

- **Decide**: At this point, you have ingested information from your network through your monitoring capability and distilled it into actionable, prioritized work. You do not make decisions based on your:
    - Corporate policy
    - Incident response plan and procedures
    - Regulatory requirements
    - Applicable laws
- **Act**: You guessed it. It is time to act. This is where you take the necessary following steps:
    - **Contain the threat**: Make sure that the threat cannot spread any further
    - **Eradicate the threat**: Remove the threat from the affected information system
    - **Recover from the threat**: Restore the information system back to a fully operational state

The following image graphically represents the OODA loop as it relates to an effectively implemented incident response capability:

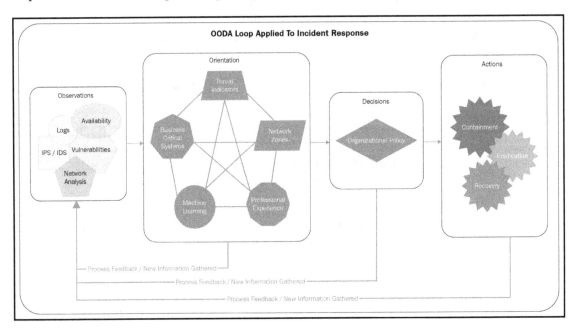

You can see that each phase in the loop feeds another, and that each phase can go back to the beginning. This represents the fact that as you go through the process you may need to go back to a state of observation. This stems from the fact that you may uncover additional information during your incident response investigation which requires you to engage in further analysis.

Incident response procedure development

Incident response procedures are a tactical component of the incident response capability, whereby the incident responder has clearly documented repeatable processes, which allow the incident responder to conduct the activities necessary to do the following:

- Detect and analyze whether a threat exists
- Contain, eradicate, and recover from a threat

When it comes to incident response procedures you will want to implement a checklist approach that allows your incident responders to have clear instructions and guidance, including all the necessary steps to conduct a specific incident response activity. The following sample is a recommended checklist that your organization should implement:

- **Emergency contact checklist**: One of the biggest issues that many organizations encounter during an incident or emergency is not knowing who to contact. In a crisis, this can cause mistakes to be made as team members run around, scream, and shout. A good checklist will clearly communicate who, what, when, why, and, how communications should be conducted during an incident response activity. A communication checklist should include:
    - Information for the entire incident response team:
        - Information security team
        - IT team (network, systems, apps, and so on)
        - Business team

- **Call tree**: Key roles for incident response and their order of contact.
- **Security analysis checklist**: An incident responder should develop checklists for the various technologies and business applications on their network. These checklists are very tactical and are designed as a guide for the incident handler to drill down deeper into the affected system. Focused areas for security analysis checklists include:
    - **Operating systems**: macOS, Windows, Linux
    - **Network services**: DNS, DHCP, Microsoft Active Directory
    - **Business applications**: Salesforce, Oracle, SAP
- **Incident handler bag checklist**: All incident responders should have a ready-to-go bag that has all the information they need to perform their duties if they were to become displaced, or needed to go to another facility to perform incident response duties. The bag should include:
    - Physical emergency contact checklist (if USB drives and laptops fail)
    - Physical copies of any other checklists or policies that are deemed mission-critical
    - An empty, lined notebook for documenting the incident
    - Necessary tools and utilities to perform incident response and forensic functions per your organization's incident response plan
    - Blank USB thumb drives
    - An incident response laptop—an organization may choose to put a laptop in each incident responder's bag or have one laptop for multiple responders to use

The following example is a simple high-level checklist that characterizes the overall incident response process. In the example, you can see that an emergency contact checklist would be used in *step 7*. The key takeaway here is that you will not have a single checklist to conduct your incident response activities. You will use multiple checklists to successfully closeout an incident:

Action	Completed
Identification (Detection and Analysis phase)	
1 Determine if an incident occurred	
2 Analyze precursors and indicators of compromise	
3 Perform information correlation	
4 Perform open source research (forums, search engines)	

5   If it is determined that an incident has occurred:
   • Begin fully documenting the investigation
   • Fully document and gather evidence	

6   Triage incident based on impact to the business/mission:
   • Recovery requirements
   • Application criticality
   • Data criticality	

7   Report the incident to:
   • Appropriate internal personnel
   • Authorized external organizations	

Remediation (Containment, Eradication, and Recovery)	
8 Acquire, preserve, secure, and document evidence	
9 Conduct necessary activities to contain the incident	
11 Identify and mitigate all vulnerabilities that were exploited	
12 Remove malware, inappropriate materials, and other components	

13	For each affected system and/or service, repeat Identification steps 2 - 3 and Remediation steps 8 – 12	
14	Restore affected system(s) to an operational state	
15	Validate that affected systems are operating normally	
Post-Incident Activity		
16	If needed, implement additional information security monitoring to detect similar activity	
17	Create after-action report	
18	Hold lesson-learned meeting	

The following is a sample incident response form that would be used to collect information related to an incident:

Sample Incident Reporting Form	
Contact information for this incident	
Name:	
Email address:	
Title:	
Program office:	
Mobile phone:	
Work phone:	
Incident description	
Provide a brief description of incident:	

Sample Incident Reporting Form

Who has been notified?

Name	Title	Email	Phone

Notes:

Sensitivity of data/information Check all that apply:

☐ Public

☐ Internal Use Only:

☐ Restricted/Confidential (privacy violation):

☐ Unknown/Other – please describe:

Public Information	Information that has been approved for public release. Unauthorized disclosure of this information will not cause a business impact. **Examples include:** • Marketing brochures • Public web pages
Internal Use Only	Information intended for use within the organization or between business partners. Unauthorized disclosure of this information may cause a business impact. **Examples include:** • Internal communications

Sample Incident Reporting Form

	• Policies • Procedures
Restricted/Confidential (privacy violation):	This information is private to the organization or is considered sensitive in nature and must be restricted to those with a legitimate business need for access. Unauthorized disclosure of this information to people without a business need for access may cause a serious business impact. Examples include: • Customer transactions • Account information • Employee performance evaluations

Provide a brief description of the data that was compromised:

Impact/Potential Impact Check all that apply:

☐ System downtime

☐ Loss/Compromise of data

☐ Damage to systems

☐ Other organizations' systems affected

☐ Violation of legislation/regulation

☐ Financial loss

☐ Damage to the integrity or delivery of critical goods, services, or information

☐ Unknown at this time

Provide a brief description of impact:

Sample Incident Reporting Form

What steps have been taken? Check all that apply:

☐ System disconnected from network

☐ Log files examined (saved and secured)

☐ Restored backup from tape

☐ Updated virus definitions and scanned system

☐ No action taken

☐ Other – please describe:

Provide a brief description of steps taken:

Incident Details

Date and time of incident:	
Physical location of system(s):	
Number of systems affected:	
Number of sites affected:	
Number of users affected:	
Has the incident been resolved?	
Provide any additional information required to properly document the incident.	

Identification – detection and analysis

Now that we have gone through the process of preparation, we are now prepared to discuss the activities around detection and analysis.

A key concept that you must understand and develop as a core component of your incident response capability is the concept of incident triage. The reality is that not all incidents are treated the same, and by using a triage approach you are able to focus on the events that are important while ignoring the noise.

The following list provides a sample of the potential attack vectors that can be used by an attacker that the incident responder will need to be prepared to respond to. Each one of the following categories is very different in how it can be exploited, and therefore will require different mechanisms to discover abnormal behavior:

- **Compromised credentials**: An attack made possible due to the harvesting of information system credentials:
  - System (OS) / service account compromises
  - User account compromises

- **Web attacks**: Attack vector that utilizes a web browser to install malware or harvest credentials:
  - Drive-by downloads
  - Cross-Site Scripting

- **Removable media**: An attack delivered via removable media:
  - USB thumb drives or DVDs left in a parking lot
  - Unsecured USB thumb drives being used by an unauthorized individual

- **Email attack**: An attack that utilizes email as a vector to deliver malware:
  - Business email compromise
  - Phishing emails / spear phishing emails

- **Loss or theft of equipment**: The loss of a device allowing an unauthorized user to have access to intellectual property:
  - Laptops without hard drive encryption
  - Mobile devices improperly configured to encrypt sensitive information

- **Information system misconfigurations**: Attack vector that takes advantage of misconfigurations in the information system:
  - Vulnerable software configurations
  - Anonymous FTP servers
  - Open proxy servers
  - Patching not maintained

- **Improper usage**: This is an incident that is generated by an authorized user performing unauthorized actions:
  - Insider threat
  - Employee exfiltration of intellectual property

An important concept related to detection and analysis is the importance of automation and properly configuring your automation tools. Tools are great to have but an improperly configured tool makes your job harder. Some thoughts to remember when configuring your automated tools include:

- **You don't need everything**: Sometimes, as information security professionals, we want to make sure that we have every aspect of an information system fully logged and fully available for us to search.

  The reality is that this costs an incredible amount of money to do, and it can make it almost impossible to find actionable information in your automated tool. Additionally, the number of false alerts is usually very high because the information is not targeted enough to perform searches against.

  Instead, perform a requirements analysis and ingest only the information you need into your incident response tools. Doing this will allow you to do more, with better data.

- **Your rules need to be good**: Many will purchase security tools and do nothing with them if the inbuilt rules are good enough. While the inbuilt rules may be good, they do not address the specific concerns related to your information system, and they certainly do not address all the work that you did with your business stakeholders to determine what was critical to the organization.

  Instead, model your information systems on the rule sets you build in your incident response tools. If you have critical information and information systems you should make sure that your automation is being used to analyze those assets.

Identification – incident response tools

We utilize people, processes, and technical tools to implement the identification phase of the incident response process, which includes detection and analysis.

Observational (OODA) technical tools

These types of tools allow the incident responder to have visibility into the network, allowing them to establish a baseline for what it normally looks like, and to easily visualize when anomalous behavior is occurring. Observational technical tools include:

- **Host and network-based intrusion prevention and intrusion detection systems (IPS/IDS)**: These tools are put in place to perform real-time monitoring of your network and server/workstation activity. These tools are typically signature-based and look for suspicious activity that matches a preconfigured signature. If a condition matches a signature the tool will either block (IPS) or alert (IDS). The open source tool examples are as follows:
    - **Suricata**: https://suricata-ids.org/
    - **OSSEC**: https://ossec.github.io/
    - **Bro IDS**: https://www.bro.org/
    - **Snort**: https://www.snort.org/

- **Security information and event management (SIEM), log analysis, and log management**: These tools provide visibility into your network, systems, and applications. As part of preparation, you will want to ensure that you have complete visibility into your information systems. The open source tool examples are as follows:
    - **Graylog**: https://www.graylog.org/download
    - **OSSIM**: https://www.alienvault.com/products/ossim
    - **Logstash**: https://www.elastic.co/products/logstash

- **Availability monitoring**: These tools monitor whether information systems are up and responsive. An availability monitoring tool could identify a pattern of outages leading to the identification of an incident. The open source tool examples are as follows:
    - **Nagios**: https://www.nagios.org/downloads/
    - **Ganglia**: https://sourceforge.net/projects/ganglia/

- **Net flow analyzers**: These tools examine the actual packets on the network and can be used to inspect for anomalous behavior. These tools can inspect any point on your network, including your boundaries. The open source tool examples are as follows:
    - **Wireshark**: https://www.wireshark.org/download.html
    - **NfSen, Nfdump**: http://nfsen.sourceforge.net/, http://nfdump.sourceforge.net/
    - **ntop**: http://www.ntop.org/get-started/download/

- **Web traffic analysis**: These tools monitor and log various kinds of traffic passed between a client and a server. These tools will allow you to analyze traffic patterns, especially in HTTP traffic streams between web browsers and web servers. The open source tool examples are as follows:
    - **IPFire**: http://www.ipfire.org/
    - **Squid proxy**: http://www.squid-cache.org/
- **Vulnerability scanners**: These tools identify vulnerable systems on your enterprise network and include potential remediation for vulnerabilities identified as part of a vulnerability scan. The open source tool example is as follows:
    - OpenVas: http://www.openvas.org/

Orientation (OODA) tools

Orientation tools help to shape our view of the tremendous amount of observational information that we have access to as part of a modern information system. These tools allow us to separate mundane information system activity from potential threats that could result in a loss of confidentiality, integrity, or availability:

- **Asset management**: These tools allow you to get a full picture regarding the pieces that make up your enterprise information systems from a network, workstation, server, software, and enterprise application perspective.

    A good asset inventory will mirror your organization's risk management program in that you will have established clear boundaries around high-risk and business-critical processes, data, and information systems. An asset management tool will help you keep the thousands of individual technology components that make up your high-risk inventory.

    Doing this allows you to focus your attention from an incident investigation perspective. From a triage perspective, if you see an event coming from a system that you know is critical to the functioning of the business you know to give this additional priority. The key is to not become complacent and only look at events coming from business-critical systems. Do not ignore other notable events. The open source tool example is as follows:

    - **Snipe-IT**: https://snipeitapp.com/download
    - **OCS Inventory**: https://www.ocsinventory-ng.org
    - **GLPI**: http://glpi-project.org
    - **Fusion Inventory**: http://fusioninventory.org

- **Threat intelligence**: Threat intelligence provides you with threat information as it relates to the following:
  - Global threats that impact indiscriminately
  - Regional threats that target a specific geographic region or country
  - Industry-specific threats that impact specific groups, such as the energy or retail sector
  - Organization-specific threats, where threat actors are specifically targeting your organization for compromise
  - Threat intelligence feeds the incident response process with **indicators of compromise** (**IOC**), which is information that can be used to provide context and help to reduce enterprise log data down to a more reasonable level
- For example:

  - A web proxy produces millions of access logs a day for internet web servers, based on requests from your organizational team members
  - Within those logs, there is a request to access a command and control server for a botnet network
  - As part of your threat intelligence toolset, you had information that allowed your logging tools to alert you that this botnet server was accessed
  - You can begin the triage process to determine if a compromise occurred

Open source tool examples:

- **IBM X-Force Exchange**: https://www.ibm.com/us-en/marketplace/ibm-xforce-exchange
- **Open IOC**: http://www.openioc.org/
- **AlienVault OTX**: https://www.alienvault.com/open-threat-exchange

Decision (OODA) tools

Decision tools allow you to ensure that you have repeatable, methodical, and trustworthy processes as it relates to your incident response capability. These tools allow you to take the triaged threat information from your observation and orientation tools and make an appropriate risk-based decision to protect your organization.

Unlike the other tools we have discussed so far, decision tools are not something you can simply download and start running against your information system. Decision tools are the policies, procedures, and plans that you put together as part of your information security and incident response programs. While there are great places on the internet to grab samples, you will quickly find that they do not address the needs of your organization. This is because you must build policy, procedures, and plans that fit into your organization's unique organizational culture, and tie into your business and mission needs and purpose. No template on the internet can do that for you. As you develop your tools that support your incident response decision-making process you must ensure that you tightly adhere to the following:

- Your organization's corporate policy
- Your organization's regulatory requirements
- Your organization's applicable laws

Remediation – containment/recovery/mitigation

Remediation is the point in the process where you, as the incident responder, engage the threat and work to protect the organization from further harm.

We are now at the point in the process where we perform the actions necessary to respond to the threat. This is made possible through the high-quality data made available through the observe and orient tools. We have taken that data and made an appropriate decision based on our organization's mission and legal requirements. With that decision, we implement the appropriate information security tools to do the following:

1. **Contain the threat**:
   - **Initially limiting damage**: Ensuring that the attacker is unable, or finds it very difficult, to cause damage to other information systems.
   - **Fully containing threat**: The reality is that as you respond to the incident you may not be able to fully contain the threat within the first few minutes of the incident. However, your goal is full containment so that you can begin the process of eradication.

2. **Eradicate the threat**:
   - During this phase of remediation, we are concerned with the complete removal of the threat from our information systems.
   - Care must be taken to fully understand the threat, ensuring that it is fully removed from the information system. Not doing this could result in the attacker still maintaining a foothold in your information system, resulting in a future outbreak based on an improperly remediated incident.

3. **Recover from the threat**:
   - Part of the incident response process must account for restoring the information system back to its fully operational capability
   - The incident response team must test to ensure the following:
     - That the information system is operating as expected and the business processing capability has resumed
     - That the threat has been completely neutralized and there are no indications that the threat has resurfaced

Remediation - incident response tools

Remediation is the point in the process where you, as the incident responder, engage the threat and work to protect the organization from further harm.

Act (Response) (OODA) tools

Tools that should be part of an effective response toolkit include:

- **Forensics tools**: These tools allow you to accurately examine digital media using processes that allow for the establishment of a legal, sound, audit trail ensuring that you can accurately do the following:
  - Identify important investigative information for backup
  - Preserve identified information for future analysis
  - Analyze preserved information to uncover facts
  - Act on facts through further investigation, response, or reporting

Open source tool examples:

- **CAINE**: http://www.caine-live.net/
- **SANS Investigative Forensic Toolkit (SIFT)**: https://digital-forensics.sans.org/community/downloads

- **Backup tools**: In most cases, it is safer to restore an environment from a backup rather than attempting to clean it after an intrusion has occurred. There is far too much risk associated with knowing if you have properly cleaned an affected device. Backup tools allow you to recover from an incident with a fully restored environment including your data.

Many of the considerations for planning the proper use of backup tools come from the concepts of business continuity and disaster recovery covered in Chapter 7, *Business Continuity/Disaster Recovery Planning*. A concept not covered in the BCDR chapter is that you need to have enough available backups to ensure that if you restore a backup, you will not be restoring backed up malware. Ensure that you have enough backup data so that you can go back in time to restore data that was available prior to an incident.

Open source tool examples:

- **Amanda: Open source backup**: http://amanda.zmanda.com/
- **Clonezilla**: http://clonezilla.org/

Post incident activity

We will cover post incident activity in the following sections.

Lessons-learned sessions

Once you have usefully closed out an incident, it is important that you conduct a lessons-learned session to determine the following:

- Where improvements need to be made in the process:
    - Do new procedures need to be created?
    - Do new alerts, signatures, and/or search parameters need to be added to automation tools?
    - Were the plans followed? Did we run around, scream, and shout?
    - Is training required?

Conducting a thorough lessons-learned session, with tasks to perform updates, will help to instill confidence that your incident response program is competent and that you are willing to address shortcomings and improve your own processes.

Once you have discovered actions, you must ensure that you complete those activities. Ensure that you develop tasks or projects as necessary to mitigate any of your discovered shortcomings in your incident response process.

Incident response plan testing

Like business continuity / disaster recovery, incident response is not something you want to test as part of an active incident. You must ensure that you adequately test your overall incident response capability on a periodic basis:

- **Active exercise**:
    - **Red team**: Utilizing information security experts that are skilled in penetrating networks you can perform activities that simulate an actual network attack.
    - **Blue team**: Utilizing your information security defenders and automation tools work to actively identify and remediate the network intrusion.
    - **Purple team**: The two teams work together rather than working as adversaries. The purple team combines the efforts of the other two teams, with the added benefit of collaboration, to dive deeper and uncover greater vulnerabilities.
- **Passive exercise**:
    - A tabletop exercise that pits the plan versus the technology
    - Individual team members work through the planning phases, testing communication
    - Team members work through scenarios and discuss what they would do versus performing the actions on the information system

Just like I mentioned in the *Lessons-learned session* section previously, if you find an issue with your incident response capability you must make sure that you properly capture the issue and develop an appropriate plan to mitigate the issue.

The following diagram sums up the content of this chapter, showing the interrelation and cycles that the various phases and components of a well-functioning incident response program follows:

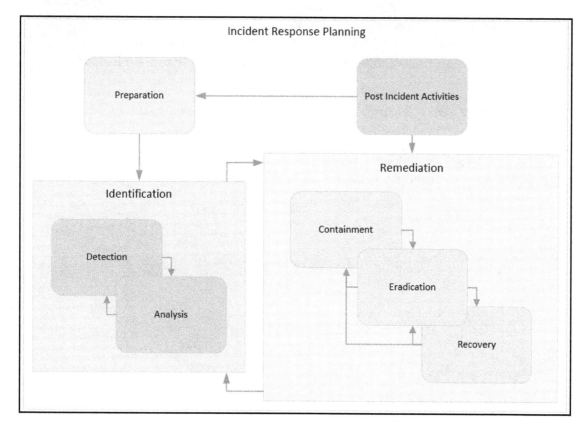

Summary

The incident response plan ensures that the information security program has the necessary people, processes, and technologies in place to respond to an information security incident against your organizational information systems.

In this chapter, you learned:

- What makes up the incident response plan and why you use one
- What is needed to establish an effective incident response plan
- Automation, tools, and techniques needed to effectively support incident response activities

In the next chapter, you will learn about the security operation center. The security operations center serves to provide visibility and responses for the enterprise network, allowing for immediate action if an attacker is detected. The security operations center is a natural extension of the incident response discussion as your security operations center is typically tasked with the implementation and monitoring of the incident response plan.

9

Developing a Security Operations Center

The **security operations center** (**SOC**) serves as your centralized view into your overall enterprise organization infrastructure and individual information systems. The security operations center's goal is to ensure that this view is as real time as possible so that your organization can identify and respond to internal and external threats as quickly as possible, helping to ensure the continued confidentiality, integrity, and availability of your organization's information systems.

Think of the SOC as the technological equivariant of the physical security controls implemented by your organization.

In this chapter, we will be discussing:

- The responsibilities of the security operations center
- Security operations center tool management
- Security operations center tool design
- Security operations center roles
- Security operations center processes and procedures
- Internal versus outsourced security operations center

From the physical security world, you have capabilities, including:

- Guard stations
- Guards
- Cameras
- Motion detectors

These capabilities serve to ensure that individuals cannot have unauthorized physical access to your building and the assets contained therein.

From the information security world, similar SOC capabilities would include:

- SOC facility
- SOC analysts
- The **security information and event management** (**SIEM**) tools
- Intrusion prevention and detection tools

The technological capabilities utilized by the SOC provide similar assurance from an information security perspective as their counterparts mentioned previously for physical security. The key difference is that the SOC is primarily interested in monitoring information systems versus physical spaces.

Responsibilities of the SOC

The SOC is responsible for the continuous identification and remediation of threats that occur on your enterprise network. If this seems familiar, it should be, as this comes from the previous chapter on incident response. Typically, it is your SOC team that will be charged with executing substantial portions of the incident response plan. Therefore, most well planned SOCs mirror much of the process that is defined in an organization's incident response plan.

Regardless of the size of your organization, the necessity to develop an effective security operations center is essential. A security operations center is an incredibly important part of your overall information security program investment and is a key component in ensuring that your organization is being properly protected from internal and external threats.

The SOC capabilities that you can implement are directly tied to your organization's personnel resources, funding, and so on. This means that a startup will have a very different looking SOC then a multi-billion dollar a year in revenue manufacturer. Regardless of your size, it is important that you determine how you will go about implementing the concepts of an SOC. If you are a small organization, determine how you can have a high level of visibility in your information system and how you will react if you find anomalies. This, of course, must be rightsized into your available resources and your business expectations.

As mentioned previously, the security operations center has similarities related to the physical security world. Most businesses, even small business, have some sort of physical alarm system and nearly all businesses have locks on the doors. The security operations center provides the necessary protections for an organization's data and information system investments. An organization should invest in their security operations center commensurate with the value of the data they are attempting to protect.

Management of security operations center tools

The SOC team must ensure that the tools used to monitor the enterprise information systems are properly secured and maintained. It will be very difficult, if not impossible to properly secure modern, complex, interconnected information systems without the aid of well-maintained and properly functioning information security tools. The SOC team must have a toolset capability at their disposal that allows them to have visibility throughout the information systems that they are responsible for monitoring.

Visibility into your organizational information systems is one of the most important aspects of a well-developed information security program. The reality is that even with a suite of well-developed security controls and a strong risk management program, intrusions will occur. How your organization responds to a future intrusion will determine whether you have a costly data exposure that could ultimately lead your organization to an untimely end. This means that your organization must pay careful attention to the selection, management, and use of the security operations center tools utilized by your organization.

Security operation center toolset design

Care must be taken when developing the overall design of your organization's SOC toolset, drawing upon the maturity developed during the implementation of your overall information security program. The development of your SOC toolset should center on what is important to your organization's missions, and ultimately being able to ensure that your organization continues to be able to exercise that mission.

You must ensure that you work with your stakeholders to determine key information such as:

- Sensitive organizational data
- Sensitive information technology assets
- Your organization's risk appetite
- Allowable business process disruption
- How information systems are interconnected and communicate with each other

Work with your organizational leaders and users to develop an understanding of important technical information such as:

- How your business applications and databases interact with each other
- How different business applications share information
- How the servers are configured that support these business applications
- How the network is configured to ensure effective communications with business applications

Understanding information such as that presented, and more, will help you to ensure that you have the necessary visibility into the aspects of your organization's network and information system. Doing this will help you to protect the assets that matter the most, allowing you to react if an internal or external threat attempts to access those assets.

Using already implemented toolsets

As part of the defense, an in-depth strategy associated with your organization's information security control implementation, you may find that you already have a wealth of tools at your disposal to properly alert to and defend yourself against threats. These are the tools that are already deployed throughout your enterprise and are used to manage your environment from the following perspectives:

- Network
- Server
- Workstation
- Application

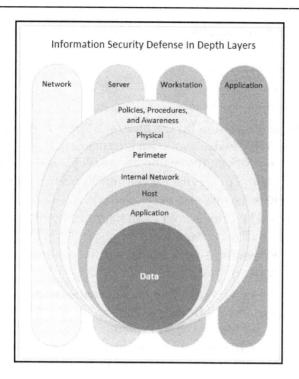

The layers of defense applied to your organization's network, servers, workstations, and applications provide protection from threats as well as reporting and alerting in the event of threatening acts on an information system. Protection and visibility that are part of the defensive layers include:

- **Policies, procedures, and awareness layer**:
    - Policies and procedures provide you with the necessary information to understand what normal looks like from business risk and technical implementation perspectives. While policies and procedures don't provide reporting or alerts, they do provide you with the information needed to ensure that you can have effective alerting.
    - Awareness ensures that you have adequately trained your leadership, general, and technical users regarding their duties as it relates to policies and procedures. This helps to further inform how we will implement alerting as our users have been trained and *should not be* violating policy.

- **Physical layer: Guards, guns, and flashlights**:
    - ID badges
    - Motion
    - Cameras
    - Motion detectors
- **Perimeter layer: Protection for the outermost part of your network**:
    - **Web proxies**: Act as an intermediary device between an internal network endpoint and an internet-based HTTP resource
    - **Denial of service prevention**: Tools that allow network resources to resist denial of service attacks
    - **SMTP proxies**: Act as an intermediary device between an internal SMTP server and an internet-based SMTP resource
    - **Firewalls**: A network device that controls outgoing and incoming network traffic
- **Internal network layer: Protection for internal enterprise's network resources where your users and applications reside**:
    - **IPSec tunnels**: Allow secure communications between devices
    - **Network access control**: Ensures that only approved devices are permitted access to the enterprise network
    - **Network segmentation**: Ensures that resources on the network can only access the resources they are entitled to access
    - **Network intrusion prevention/detection systems**: Ensure that suspicious traffic is analyzed and, if necessary, blocked on the network to prevent an intrusion by an attacker
- **Host layer: Protections for server and workstation operating system**:
    - **Operating system's security controls**: This is the appropriate implementation of security controls throughout the operating system.
    - **Malware tools**: Tools that detect and eliminate malware from the host.
    - **Host intrusion prevention/detection system**: Ensures that suspicious traffic is analyzed and if necessary blocked on the host to prevent an intrusion by an attacker.
    Vulnerability management system.

- **Application layer: Protection for enterprise web applications**:
    - **Application reverse proxies**: Act as an intermediary between an internal web resource and internet or external user
    - **Security Assertion Markup Language (SAML)**: Allows internal identity services to be extended to other services inside and outside of the enterprise network
    - **Single sign on**: Allows for a single set of credentials to be utilized throughout the enterprise network
    - **Web application firewall**: Provides protection for web vulnerabilities in enterprise web applications
- **Data layer: Protection against data abuse**:
    - **Information rights management**: Allows data to be secured inside and outside of the network, typically implementing a call home mechanism to verify file permissions before allowing access
    - **Database security**: Implementation of appropriate security controls from a database perspective
    - **Mobile device encryption**: Ensuring that organizational data is properly encrypted across mobile devices
    - **Data loss prevention (DLP)**: Tools that allow organizational data protection polices to be automated and enforced at that network level

Security operations center roles

To have an effective security operation center, it is critical that you implement the necessary personnel roles to properly operate and maintain the environment. In the following list, you will find the personnel roles needed to fully implement a security operations center. Do not get hung up on the names of the roles if they do not match those in your organization. Each organization will have its own naming convention derived from the organization's culture:

- **Security operations center analysts**:
    - **Tier one**: More junior information security analyst with a couple of years' experience in the information security field. Possesses a basic knowledge of networking, systems, and applications:
        1. Conducts information security tool monitoring
        2. Conducts basic investigations and mitigations
        3. Opens tickets

- **Tier two**: Poses a stronger knowledge of the information security tools used by the SOC as well as a deeper understanding of networking, systems, and applications:
  1. Deeper investigative techniques
  2. Threat mitigation
  3. Recommends changes to information systems
- **Tier 3**: Is stronger in SOC and IT skills than the tier two analysts and typically has skills in forensics, malware analysis, threat intelligence, and more:
  1. Advanced investigations
  2. Malware analysis
  3. Threat hunting
  4. Counter intelligence
  5. Forensics

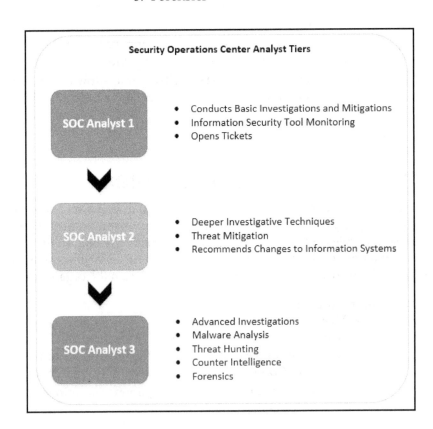

Security Operations Center Analyst Tiers

SOC Analyst 1
- Conducts Basic Investigations and Mitigations
- Information Security Tool Monitoring
- Opens Tickets

SOC Analyst 2
- Deeper Investigative Techniques
- Threat Mitigation
- Recommends Changes to Information Systems

SOC Analyst 3
- Advanced Investigations
- Malware Analysis
- Threat Hunting
- Counter Intelligence
- Forensics

- **Serve as primary team member performing incident response**: It includes preparation, detection, analysis, containment, eradication, recovery, and post-incident activities:

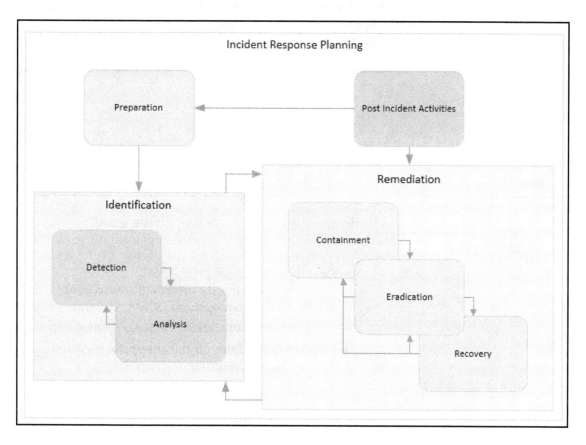

- As required, this role may additionally:
  - Implement additional information security tools in support of the security operations center. Most complex implementations would be performed by a security engineer.
  - Create new operational procedures related to threat detection, analysis, containment, eradication, and recovery.

- **Information security engineers**:
    - Responsible for the systems development/engineering life cycle from `Chapter 3`, *Preparing for Information and Data Security*, which includes initiation, requirements analysis, design, implementation, testing, operations and Maintenance, and disposition of security operations tools:

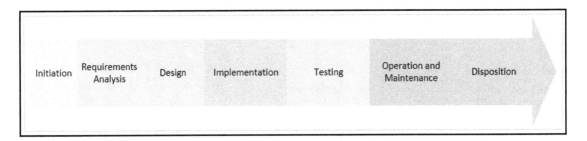

| Initiation | Requirements Analysis | Design | Implementation | Testing | Operation and Maintenance | Disposition |

- Typically, the security engineer will support the security operations center as well as the enterprise organization. As a result, they:
    - Develop capabilities for the SOC, such as:
        - **Security information and event management** (**SIEM**) systems
        - Vulnerability management systems
    - Develop capabilities for the enterprise such as:
        - Firewall and IDS/IPS designs
        - Implementation of security requirements within enterprise projects

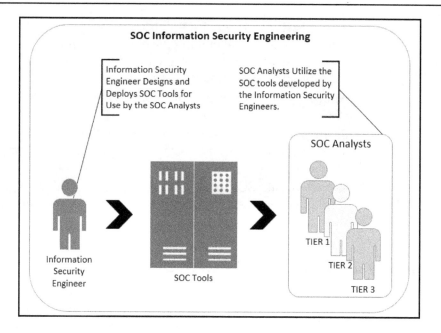

- **Security operations center manager**:
    - The security operations center manager is responsible for the overall management of the SOC and its day-to day-operations. Additionally, the SOC manager is responsible for:
        - Creating a new SOC-related policy.
        - Creating and approving new SOC-related procedures and processes.
        - Managing security operations center analysts. Typically, the SOC analysts work directly for the SOC manager.
        - Coordinating with information security engineers. Typically, the information security engineers work within a different part of the information security program. However, there is nothing precluding an SOC from having its own information security engineers.

- **Chief information security officer (CISO):**
    - Is responsible for developing the overall organizational information security program, which includes the organization's security operations center
    - Approves all new policies, procedures, and processes related to the SOC
    - Ensures that the SOC capability aligns with the organization's information security risk management program and compliance programs
    - Communicates SOC threat data to organizational management in support of the overall information security program goals

Log or information aggregation

A key design attribute for an effective SOC monitoring capability is logs, and lots of them. Your design will include a mechanism to aggregate and correlate the logging information that you are gathering so that you can triage and prioritize information that may lead to the identification of an active threat on your network. When establishing this capability, ensure that you are:

Receiving logging events from their original source or a logging service that allows the logs to be forwarded to their destination without the log data being altered:

- If the log data is changed in transit from the log source, your ability to have accurate visibility into your information system will be seriously degraded
- You will want to include logs and information from throughout your organization's information systems to ensure that you are receiving the maximum amount of visibility possible:
    - Security-relevant log events from on-premise infrastructure including active directory, database servers, file server, firewall, Domain Name System, email servers, web servers, and so on
- Security-relevant log events from the cloud and third-party hosting providers, including:
    - Cloud providers such as Amazon AWS, Google for Business, Microsoft Azure, and so on
    - Third-party web providers, server and workstation virtualization services, and so on

- Vulnerability data from your vulnerability management system
- Alerts from your host and network-based intrusion prevention and intrusion detection systems (IPS/IDS)
- Real-time network information from net flow analyzers
- Alerts from web proxies
- Threat intelligence from third-party and organizational sources

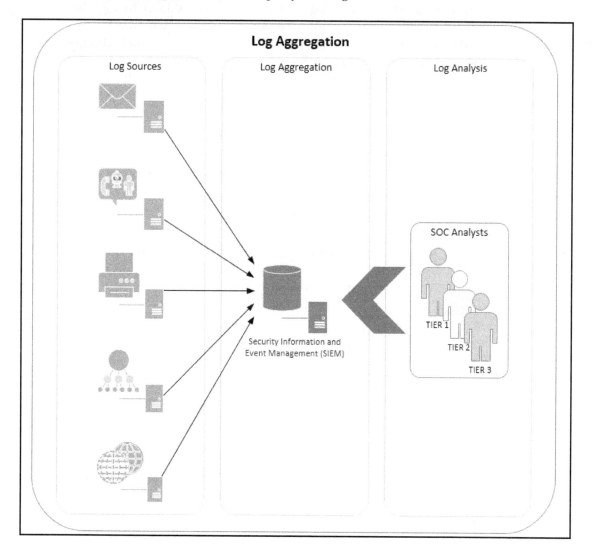

Log or information analysis

Once you have visibility into your production environment by gaining access to information system data and log sources, it is now time to begin performing log reduction and log analytics:

- **Log reduction**: Implementing log reduction takes all of the available information that can be understood from a log source and reduces it down to only the information necessary to determine if a threat exists on the network
- **Log analytics**: The automated and human interactions associated with log review and the work necessary to establish analytics automation:
    - The **indicator of compromise** (**IOC**) analysis, such as:
        - Internet domain names
        - File hashes
        - Geographic location irregularities
        - IP addresses
        - Privileged user account anomalous behavior
        - Potential data exfiltration
    - Designing, testing, and implementing correlation rules for events and alerts
    - Conducting triage on events and alerts generated via correlation rules:
        - Establish threat attribution
        - Document details related to the threat
    - Communicate findings, moving the incident response activity from the identification phase to the remediation phase

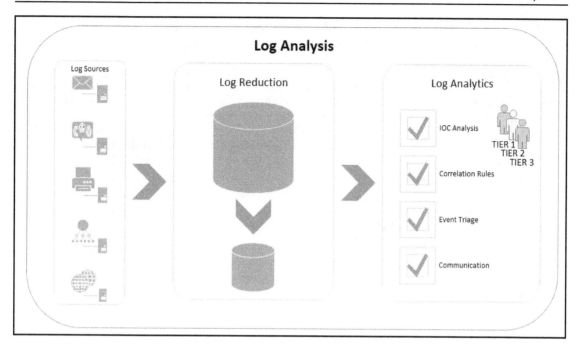

Processes and procedures

The key component to an effectively-run SOC is well-thought-out processes and procedures. An SOC must be able to implement effective identification and remediation activities the same way all the time. Effective processes and procedures ensure that this is carried out in a repeatable and reliable fashion.

Key process and procedure categories are needed to ensure an effectively managed and operating SOC mirror the incident response life cycle and include:

- **Identification**:
    - Detection
    - Analysis
- **Remediation**:
    - Containment
    - Eradication
    - Recovery

The following is a sample process that identifies the parties and their duties if confronted with cross-site scripting vulnerability being identified on an organizational web application:

Process steps	Role
• Identifies or receives a report of an XSS vulnerability	SOC analyst

• Documents the identification/report as an incident:
  ○ XSS vulnerability identified and includes the following information in the tracking form:
    ▪ Vulnerable site/script (URL)
    ▪ Source of the report/identification
	SOC analyst

• Notifies the SOC manager of the incident through email	SOC analyst
• Identifies the owner of the website and the responsible manager	SOC manager

• Opens a help desk ticket with the following standard recommendations:
  ○ Website owner to perform the following:
    ▪ Analyze/validate the reported XSS vulnerability
    ▪ Correct/remove any exploitable pages/scripts from the site
	SOC analyst

• Remediates the vulnerability	Website owner
• Validates that vulnerability has been closed	SOC analyst
• Closes the incident when notified by the website owner/developer	SOC analyst

Identification – detection and analysis

Being able to collect an incredible amount of log data from your organization's information systems is ultimately not the goal of the SOC. The goal is to take this information and, in a repeatable fashion, effectively analyze available information to detect whether an information security threat exists on the enterprise network.

This is where indicators of compromise are used to inform your information security tools (via correlation rules) and personnel to look for threats on the enterprise network. Indicators of compromise can be found within:

- System events:
    - Network
    - Applications
- Firewall connections

- User activity
- Suspicious system file or registry changes
- Untimely information system usage
- DDoS activity, and so on

Being able to properly handle events will depend primarily on the security operations center's ability to properly triage and categorize events so that you can effectively prioritize SOC activities, ensuring that critical threats are handled before less critical activities are started. As mentioned throughout this book, it is important to ensure that the SOC triage and categorization processes are tied tightly to business needs so that any investigations that are started are initially focused on business-critical concerns.

Processes implemented by the security operations center analysts during this phase include:

- **Tier one**:
    - Review events that have the highest severity or criticality:
        - This information will be defined in the organization's SIEM tool
    - Establish a help desk ticket once it has been determined that an event requires further investigation:
        - If the event requires further investigation, it will be escalated to the tier two SOC analyst

- **Tier two**:
    - Conducts a thorough investigation and triage of the event, fully documenting the identified threat for remediation
    - Information that must be documented includes:
        - Date and time of event/incident
        - Points of contact throughout event investigation:
        - Name, email, phone number, and so on
        - Description of event/incident
        - Individuals notified
        - Identification of VIPs and executives
        - Data sensitivity
        - Potential impact of event/incident
        - Steps taken as part of the investigation
        - Physical location of system(s)

- Number of systems affected
- Number of sites affected
- Number of users affected
- Has the incident been resolved?
- Provide any additional information required to properly document the event/incident

Events versus alerts versus incidents

The concepts of events, alerts, and incidents are integrated into the identification processes of a well-functioning security operations center:

- An event is a change to the expected behavior of an:
  - Information system
  - Process
  - Environment
  - Workflow
  - Person
- An alert is provided by an information security monitoring system such as a SIEM to identify an event or combination of events
- An incident is a malicious event that has some level of business impact and must be remediated

False positive versus false negative/true positive versus true negative

- **False positive:**
  - A false positive is a false alarm
  - This is the state when an information security tool identifies an information system processing as an attack but, it is expected information system behavior

- **False negative:**
  - Most dangerous condition
  - A false negative is when an information security tools identifies attack behavior as normal information system operations
  - In this condition, the attack is unseen by the information security tools
  - This is one of the reasons for a good, in-depth defense strategy. One tool that reports a false negative may be caught by another tool

- **True positive:**
  - Properly working information security tool
  - This is when attack behavior is identified as attack behavior by the information system
  - While many tools can catch millions of threats with out-of-the-box behavior, the information security professional must constantly tune their information security tools to ensure that a true positive state is maintained

- **True negative:**
  - Properly working information security tool
  - This is when an information security tool properly identifies information system behavior as acceptable

Remediation – containment/eradication/recovery

Here is where we come to the true purpose of establishing a security operations center—containment, eradication, and recovery from external and internal threats to your organization. Being able to respond to a threat rapidly will spell the difference between an easily contained versus a highly damaging incident.

Your remediation strategy is also very much tied to your business's mission, and the steps that you take to remediate a threat can be very different from one organization to another.

Regardless of your organization's business strategy, your SOC team must ensure that they effectively:

- **Contain the threat**: Ensuring that the attacker is unable to or finds it very difficult to cause damage on other information systems

- **Eradicate the threat**: The complete removal of the threat from your information system
- **Recover from the threat**: Restore the information system back to its fully operational capability

Strategies used as part of this phase include:

- Updating and/or patching to close vulnerabilities in your network, servers, workstations, and applications
- Updating system access to remove an attacker's privileges
- Changing network access to disrupt attacker communications
- Reimage or reset devices to ensure the removal of attacker software
- Ensure that SOC monitoring capabilities are properly tuned to ensure efficient detection based on lessons learned
- Ensure that additional security controls are applied to the information systems as needed to prevent future attacks

The following is a sample security operations center **standard operating procedure** (**SOP**), which provides the steps an organization could use to block network access to a threat as part of normal operations or in response to an incident:

Process steps	Role
1. Identifies or receives report of malicious IP addresses or URLs	SOC analyst

2. Processes the identification or report by:
  a. Creating a helpdesk ticket
  b. Notifying the SOC manager of the ticket
	SOC analyst

3. Analyzes the identification or report and determines the systems that require updates	SOC analyst
4. Generates a list of the IP addresses/URLs to be added to the appropriate network blocking tool	SOC analyst
5. Ensures that tracking databases and information security tools are updated with IOC information	SOC analyst
6. Ensures that all appropriate business and IT stakeholders are informed of the impending information system update	SOC analyst

For a firewall block	
7. Generates a list of the IP addresses to be added to the firewall	SOC analyst
8. Opens a helpdesk ticket for a firewall IP address block request providing list of IP addresses to be blocked	SOC analyst
9. Applies the suspect IP address to the firewall and notifies the SOC when actions are complete	FW admin
For a web proxy block	

For a web proxy block	
10. Generates a list of the IP addresses/URLs to be added to the firewall	SOC analyst
11. Opens a helpdesk ticket for a web proxy IP address/URL block request providing list of IP addresses/URLs to be blocked	SOC analyst
12. Applies the suspect IP address/URLs to the web proxy and notifies the SOC when actions are complete	Web proxy admin

Security operations center tools

The security operations center utilizes the tools defined in the incident response chapter of this book, and those tools should be used as a reference to build out the technical capability of a SOC.

Key tools to highlight for SOC use include:

- **Security information and event management (SIEM)**: Provides deep visibility into your network, systems, and applications. The SIEM is really where the magic happens for the SOC. The SIEM is the tool that ties your other security tools such as malware analysis and intrusion prevention tools into a unified system that can produce very intricate events and alerts. In turn, this capability can serve to provide the necessary ingredients to conduct identification and remediation activities.

- **Host and network-based intrusion prevention and intrusion detection systems (IPS/IDS)**: Perform real-time monitoring of your network and server/workstation activity.
- **Vulnerability scanners**: Identify vulnerable systems on your enterprise network and include potential remediation recommendations for vulnerabilities identified as part of a vulnerability scan.
- **Net flow analyzers**: Examine the actual packets on the network and can be used to inspect for anomalous behavior.

Security operations center advantages

The advantages of SOC are as follows:

SOC	MSSP
Ability to implement tools that fit your requirements. Full control over staff resources.	MSSPs provide the tools they provide. Typically, no custom tool selections are available. MSSP resources are typically spread across multiple customers.
Ability to fully customize information security tools.	Typically limited, no customization is available.
Full control over your organization's log data for analysis and compliance.	Log data is stored offsite at the vendor facility.

An important point that an organization must consider when planning out their SOC capability is whether to purchase a full complement of information security tools, or to go down the route of an MSSP.

An MSSP provides an attractive option for a small business, as the MSSP provider runs and operates the information security infrastructure for the organization. Additionally, the MSSP providers provide the monitoring capability of the security analyst, and depending on how much money you want to spend, can completely replace your organization's security operations center capabilities.

The key point to call out here is how much money you want to spend. Replacing the capabilities described in this chapter and the Chapter 8, *Incident Response Planning,* would result in a very expensive vendor bill indeed.

The first thing you need to do when looking at an MSSP is going back to the business requirements and planning.

Clearly define your requirements by asking yourself questions such as:

- What are you trying to achieve with an MSSP?
  - Are you attempting to fully replace an SOC?
  - Are you trying to implement a log monitoring capability?
- Can your information security needs be outsourced?
  - Information security data is sensitive, can this information be in the possession of a third party?
- What are your monitoring requirements?
  - Can your internet service support the bandwidth for external monitoring?

MSSP advantages

The advantages of MSSP are as follows:

MSSP	SOC
Cheaper to establish assuming you fully understand your requirements.	Large investment in hardware, software, and expertise.
Easier to establish a 24x7x365 SOC capability.	Incredible management overhead associated with overlapping shifts and human resources.
Access to qualified information security personnel through vendor.	Must source and hire SOC staff.

Summary

In this chapter, we learned that the **security operations center** (**SOC**) serves as your centralized view into your overall enterprise organizational infrastructure.

In this chapter, we discussed:

- What the responsibilities of the security operations center include
- Management of security operations center tools
- Design considerations for security operations center tools
- Personnel roles in the security operations center
- Processes and procedures required to run a security operations center
- Internal versus outsourced security operations center

In the next chapter, we will discuss information security architecture concepts and implementation steps towards implementing an effective, well-integrated information security architecture program.

10

Developing an Information Security Architecture Program

Information security architecture establishes rigorous and comprehensive policies, procedures, and guidelines around the development and operationalization of an information security architecture across the enterprise information technology deployed within an organization.

An organization's information security architecture must be tightly aligned with the organization's business mission in order to be successful. Establishing an information security architecture program that ultimately hampers the mission success will result in the architecture being ignored and the organization's risk level increasing.

When aligning your information security architecture with your business mission, you should ask yourself similar questions to those that you asked throughout the development of your information security program:

- What is your organization's business risk appetite?
    - How much risk is your organization willing to tolerate?
    - How much is your organization willing to spend to reduce risk?
- How mature is your organization?
    - Is your organization a startup running out of Office 365 or Google Apps for business?
    - Is your organization a 40-year-old manufacturer with 15,000 employees and 200 locations?

- Is your organization's information technology centralized or decentralized?
- How does your organization approach foundational IT/hygiene issues?
  - Topics:
    - Asset discovery and management
    - Secure configurations
    - Account privilege restriction
    - Patching
- Is your organization mature, and does it work to ensure the IT systems are maintained?
- Are IT solutions built and forgotten about until they break?
- Is your organization somewhere in between? Determine where your organization sits.

Understanding answers to questions like these will help you to ensure that your information security architecture program is well targeted to the organization. These questions will also allow you to establish plans to adjust your information security architecture program as your organization matures.

Information security architecture and SDLC/SELC

To establish a successful security architecture program, it is extremely important to ensure that you are well integrated into your organizational systems development/engineering life cycle.

The SDLC/SELC lifecycle is used to ensure consistently repeatable processes as part of an engineering and/or development project. The information security architect must ensure that these life cycles are integrated into these repeatable processes and that they are working with the IT and development engineering and developer teams. The organization uses the processes that make up the SDLC/SELC to improve predictability and quality as part of the engineering or development process. The SDLC/SELC process combined with strong participation from the information security will help to ensure a well-designed system that has security built in to it from project initiation.

A typical SELC/SDLC process contains the following phases:

1. **Initiation phase**: During the initiation phase of a project, the organization defines the need for an information system. Information security planning begins in the initiation phase where the information security architect works with the project team to understand the security considerations that will need to be applied to the system:

    - **Information security architect role**: Work with project stakeholders to educate them on the role of information security and ensures:
        - For this to be best communicated, it is recommended that formalized education and training be developed to properly communicate the role of the information security architect to the project stakeholders and team members. The training does not need to be voluminous, but it should be developed to ensure that the message being communicated to the project team is repeatable and conforms to the vision and goals of the business and information security program management.
    - Work with project management to ensure that they are included in all appropriate project activities.
    - Conduct an initial security analysis of the project, considering the following elements and goals:
        - Purpose and description of the information system
        - Determine compliance requirements
        - Document key information system and project roles
        - Define the expected user types
        - Document interface requirements
        - Document external information systems access
        - Conduct a business impact assessment
        - Conduct an information data categorization
    - The purpose of the initial security analysis is to capture as much information about the project's goals upfront so that you can begin immediately making security recommendations. The project team may not have all of the answers at the beginning. That is perfectly acceptable, and is expected. As the information security architect, you will mature this information as the project matures, allowing you to have a well-documented view into the business and operational aspects of the information system that you are helping to design.

2. **Requirements analysis phase**: During the requirements analysis phase, the information security architect works with users and business stakeholders to develop the requirements necessary for the new system. It is the job of the information security architect to ensure that security requirements are included for the new system and that they are given high priority.
    - **Information security architect role**: Provide information security requirements to the project team for inclusion into the overall project's requirements.
      The security requirements should be tailored to the needs of the information system being implemented:
        - If the information system does not implement a technology, then the security requirements should not include a requirement for the unused technology
        - The information security architect should be prepared to discuss the requirements with the project team and to answer questions now, during the requirements phase, and at any point in the system's development.

3. **Design phase**: During the design phase, the requirements that where gathered during the requirements analysis phase are used to construct the new system. The role of the information security architect in this phase is to ensure that the correct information security controls are implemented as part of the system design. The design phase can be further broken down into subphases where the engineering team develops the following:
    - **Concept of operation**: A document that describes the characteristics of a system from a user perspective. This document is used to communicate how the system will operate to business stakeholders.
    - **High-level design**: A document that describes the logical components of a system and how they will interact. This document includes data flows and a description of how part of the system will interconnect.
    - **Detailed design**: A document that takes the high-level design and applies the specific configurations and costs that will be part of the system.
    - **Proof of concept system**: A proof of concept system takes the detailed design and implements a system that can be used to determine whether the design system meets the user and business stakeholder requirements. Often, the proof of concept is a scaled-down version of the proposed system to test functionality without incurring the full cost of the final system.

- **Information Security Architect role**:
  - The information security architect will work closely with the engineering and development teams during this phase to ensure that information security requirements are implemented in the form of operational, management, and technical security controls.
  - The information security architect is responsible for ensuring that the final system design properly implements the organization's information security requirements, and that they are functioning as expected.
  - The information security architect will work with the engineering and design teams to develop mitigating security controls for any information security requirements that cannot be fully implemented.

4. **Implementation phase**: During the implementation phase, the project team builds the production information system based on the design defined in the previous phase. The role of the information security architect is to ensure that the designed security controls are properly implemented and working.

  - **Information security architect role**: The information security architect ensures that the finalized design is properly translated into the implemented production system.
    The information security architect works with the engineering and development teams to work through any production implementation issues that may necessitate a deviation from design:
    - Any changes that need to be made to the information system at implementation will be developed with the information systems security requirements in mind

5. **Testing phase**: During the testing phase, the project team executes an agreed-upon test plan to ensure that the system functions as expected. The information security architect must ensure that that the implemented security controls work as expected. If any deficiencies are discovered, the security control must be identified and flagged for repair.
  - **Information security architect role**: The information security architect will develop the security testing documentation for the information system.

- The testing document addresses operational, management, and technical security controls as they relate to people, the process, and technology.
  Ensure that all necessary compliance requirements are met.
  Any deficient security controls will be flagged for immediate repair or will be mitigated through a planned implementation.

6. **Operations and maintenance phase**: During this phase, the system is in production and is under configuration management. The information security architect must ensure that any recent changes to the system are thoroughly examined for their impact to the security controls that were applied during the implementation phase:
   - **Information security architect role**: The role of the information security architect does not end once the information system is in place. The information security architect:
     - Advises the information system owner as needed on the continuing security posture of the information systems
     - Reviews and provides recommendations regarding information system changes
     - Develops any necessary security controls for the information system if its functionality or scope changes

7. **Disposition phase**: During the disposition phase, the useful life of the system has been reached and the business has decided to decommission the system. It is the responsibility of the information security architect to ensure that the system has been properly archived and sanitized in accordance with organizational policy and applicable laws.
   - **Information security architect role**: The information security architect validates that all information has been removed from the information system in a way that resists forensic retrieval.
     It validates that any required data is saved so that it can be used by the organization in the future after the information system has been decommissioned.

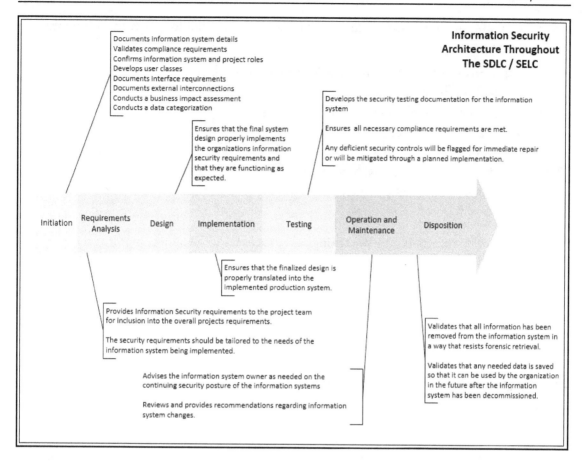

Conducting an initial information security analysis

To properly inform your decision making, as an information security architect in support of a technology project, you must be able to determine what the business and technology-related goals are for the information system being designed.

Establishing a process such as an initial information security analysis at project initiation will allow you, as the information security architect, to gather the necessary information to properly support your project and provide the most relevant guidance possible.

As part of an initial information security analysis, you will want to gather the following information:

- Purpose and description of the information system
- Compliance requirements
- Key information system and project roles
- Expected user types
- Interface requirements
- External information systems access
- Business impact assessment
- Information categorization

 An important note regarding this process is to recognize that it is referred to as an initial information security analysis. You may not be able to get all your questions answered during project initiation, and this is perfectly acceptable. However, what the process gives you is a framework to work with so that you can begin gathering the information in order for you to properly advise your project and business stakeholders.

Purpose and description of the information system

Clearly document the purpose of the system from a business perspective. In the example of a document management system, you would want to show what business need is being fulfilled. If your organization is utilizing a project management framework then you can use the information that will come out of the project chartering process to obtain this information. Otherwise, you will need to interview the business and IT stakeholders to gather this information.

- **Business purpose**: Implement a document management system to store manufacturing plans and diagrams in a secure and searchable fashion.
- **System description**: If your organization knows how they are going to implement the business purpose statement then you will want to document this now. For example, if your organization uses SharePoint and they intend to use SharePoint to satisfy the business purpose, then document the technology and other facts that are available:

- This section describes the system in narrative form using non-technical terms (tech speak):
    - The technology used should be clearly defined-in this case, SharePoint. While SharePoint is the product being implemented, this is not considered a technical term.
- Will the capability be hosted internally or outsourced?
- How does the business unit plan on using this capability?
- What is the high-level proposed system architecture? Include an architecture drawing that includes (if applicable):
    - Information system's subsystem
    - Interfaces to external systems
    - System hardware architecture
    - System software architecture
    - Storage architecture
    - Backup/disaster recovery architecture
    - Internal communications architecture
    - User inputs
    - User output

The key take away here is to develop a high-level architecture drawing that will help you to better:

- Communicate the various aspects of the information system to all stakeholders
- Verify with the project stakeholders that you accurately understand the system
- Add information security controls to show the interaction between the information system and security controls.

- Identify the functions and, if possible, the system elements that fall within the security boundary for the information system.

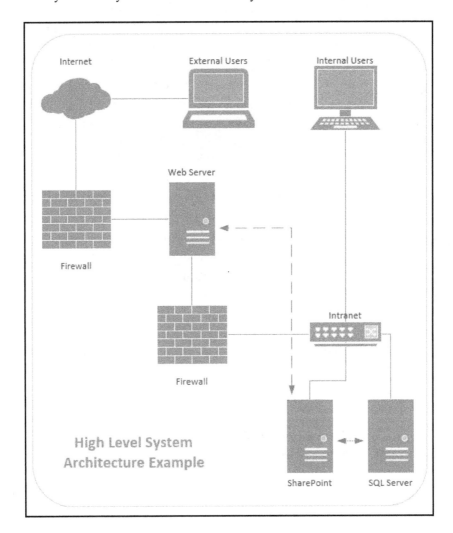

Determining compliance requirements

Prior to providing information security architecture guidance for your information system, you must look at your organization's regulatory and compliance requirements, making sure that you are building a set of security requirements that results in a secure and compliant information system.

The compliance requirements that an organization needs to follow have a significant effect on the overall shaping of an information system. The requirements imposed by various laws and compliance frameworks vary depending on the law and the framework, and it is critically important that you understand your framework in order to ensure that your organization can successfully continue to do business.

The services provided by your information system have a great deal to do with the potential mix of compliance requirements that your system must adhere to.

For example, take the example of a POS system located within a gift shop of a US federal government facility:

- In this case, an organization would typically be responsible for adhering to the compliance standards associated with the following:
    - **Federal Information Security Modernization Act**: Because they are a US federal government agency
    - **Payment Card Industry Data Security Standard**: Because they accept credit cards

> This is a very simple example and assumes that the agency is running the gift shop and not a third party.

- In this case, there is a stacking of compliance standards, which brings in complexity and special considerations from an information security architecture perspective.

Compliance standards

- **The Sarbanes-Oxley Act (SOX)**: US public companies, public accounting firms
- **Payment Card Industry Data Security Standard**: PCI-DSS: Credit card companies, retailers, any other entity that handles payment card information
- **The Gramm-Leach-Bliley Act (GLB)**: Securities firms, insurance companies, banks, brokers, lenders, and other financial institutions
- **Electronic Fund Transfer Act**: Merchants, financial institutions that provide EFT services or manage consumer accounts

- **Fair and Accurate Credit Transaction Act (FACTA)**: Financial institutions, credit reporting agencies, credit bureaus, and creditors
- **Federal Information Security Management Act (FISMA)**: US federal agencies
- **Health Insurance Portability and Accountability Act (HIPAA)**: Health plans, health care providers, and organizations that manage personal health information
- **European Union Data Protection Directive**: European business or non-European businesses that export data to another country

Documenting key information system and project roles

As information security architect, it is your role to determine the individuals that will hold key roles in the successful execution of the information system project and those individuals that will be responsible for the systems management once it is in production.

Understanding who is responsible for the various functions of the information system will be very important to you as you work to:

- Understand the purpose of the information system
- Understand who is responsible for the information system
- Understand how the information system is being constructed

Project roles

The project roles are the individuals who are typically responsible for carrying the information system from initiation to implementation:

- **Project manager:** The individual responsible for project delivery:
  - Develops the information system project plan
  - Leads and manages the project team
  - Recruits and manages project staff
  - Manages delivery of project deliverables
  - Assigns tasks to project team members
  - Provides status updates to project stakeholders

- **Project team members**: Individuals that support the delivery of the project. Project team members support the project on one or more tasks throughout the life of the project. Project team members may be:
    - Business or technical staff from the organization
    - External consultants or in-house team members
    - Team member roles could change throughout the life of the project
- **Project sponsor**: The business manager responsible for project success
    - Makes business decisions related to the information system
    - Approves the budget for the information system
    - Ensures resource availability for the project manager
    - Communicates the goals of the project throughout the organization
- **Executive sponsor**: The senior business leader responsible for supporting and championing the project throughout the organization:
    - Ultimately responsible for the project from an organizational perspective
    - Establishes and approves changes to the scope of the project
    - Provides funding for the project
    - Signs off on the final delivery of project deliverables

Information system roles

The information system roles are those roles that are tied to the business management of the system as well as the continued operations of the system's past implementation:

- **System owner**: The system owner is responsible for the management and ongoing maintenance of the information system. The information system may be:
    - Owned by the system owner (the data owner and system owner are the same)
    - Owned by a separate data owner
    - Owned by multiple data owners (data may be comingled or enclaved)

The system owner is responsible for:

- Implementation of organization-wide policies, standards, and baselines (this includes security policy)
- Establishing information system-specific policies, standards, and baselines

- Ensuring that everyone that uses the information system adheres to established policies, standards, and baselines for the information system

- **Data owner**: Is the data owner is responsible for establishing policies, standards, and baselines around how data will be used:
    - They establish rules for data usage and protection
    - They work with the information system owner to develop a secure platform for data access that meets organizational requirements
    - The data owner decides who may have access to information and what privileges a user has regarding access to data
- **Administrator**: The administrator adds and removes users to the information system. An admin also assigns permission within the information system. They are also expected to:
    - Follow a least-privileged principle
    - Execute IT-related functions to maintain the health of the information system

The following is a sample form that can be used to document the project and information system roles:

Role	Name	Title	Phone	Email
Project Roles				
Project Manager				
Project Team Member ... (add lines as needed)				
Project Sponsor				
Executive Sponsor				
Business Analyst				
Information System Roles				
System Owner				
Data Owner				
Administrator ... (add lines as needed)				

Defining the expected user types

Define all expected user types, including:

- General information system users
- External business partners
- External users/customers
- System administrators (manage infrastructures)
- Application administrators (manage web application and APIs)

For each user type, identify:

- Where the user will be accessing the information system:
  - Internal network
  - VPN
  - Internet
- Identify the client software utilized by each class of users:
  - Is the application a web application/browser-based?
  - Does the application require a thick client?
  - Identify any specific client access requirements.
    - IP addresses
    - URLs
    - TCP ports

The following is an example of a completed user type collection form where you have identified the user type and the mechanisms used to provide access to the underlying information system:

User type	Access type	Client software	IP address	TCP port	URL
General user	Internal network	Web browser	N/A	N/A	https://thewebapp
External business partner	Internet	Web browser	N/A	N/A	https://thewebapp
Customers	Internet	Web browser	N/A	N/A	https://thewebapp

System administrator	VPN	Windows operating system tools	10.0.0.1	42	N/A
Application administrator	Internal network	Thick client	10.0.0.2	24	N/A

Documenting interface requirements

Describe the various interfaces utilized by the information system to perform its information processing, including:

- **Interface overview**:
    - Describe the interface functionality
    - Define key hardware and software components related to the interface
- **Functional description**:
    - Describe the operations performed by the interface
    - Describe how the end users interact with the interface
    - Describe the events that trigger the movement of information through the interface
- **Data transfer**:
    - Describe how data is moved along the component systems of the interface
    - Describe how connectivity among the systems will be implemented
    - Describe the type of packaging or messaging of data that will be used to transfer data
- **Transactions**:
    - Describe the types of transactions that will be used to move data along the component systems of the interface being defined

The preceding process should be followed for each interface being documented for the information system in question. This activity is very important in that it allows you as the information security architect to have a full understanding of how data moves between systems and with the various types of users of the information system.

Documenting external information systems access

Ensure that you identify all other systems that interface with the information system that you are currently supporting. For each interface:

- Identify the interface name
- Identify the purpose of the interface and any specific notes concerning the interface
- Identify the direction of the data transfer
- Identify the interfacing system and the owner of the interfacing system

The following is a sample form you can use to capture this information:

Interface name	Purpose/notes	Direction	Interfacing system	System owner of interfacing information system

Conducting a business impact assessment

The business impact assessment is a key component of ensuring that information security architecture properly accounts for information system availability, backup, and disaster recovery requirements. With the business impact assessment, you are seeking to gather all the necessary information to develop an adequate information security architecture that will satisfy the business/mission owner's requirements.

Inputs to the BIA

Having actionable correct data from your business is critical to conducting an effective business impact assessment:

- **Business process supported**: Clearly identify the business process that is supported by the information system.
- **Business impact**: How would the business be impacted if the information system were to become unavailable?

- **Information systems utilized**: Identify the specific component of the information system, or note the whole information system if there are no special subsystems to identify.
- **Allowable outage**: How long can the business go without the information system being available?
- **Recovery priority**: Identify the priority tier that the information system should be placed in for recovery.

The following is a sample form that can be used to catalog business processes related to the information system being analyzed:

Business process	Impact	Allowable outage	Recovery priority	Software	Hardware	Dependencies/interfaces

Conducting an information categorization

The information security architect must work with the business and project stakeholders to properly categorize the information that will be used by the information system being analyzed.

Information categorization will aim to answer the following questions:

- What information assets will be processed by the information system?
- What is the value of those assets to your organization?
- What will it take to properly secure those assets in a way that is commensurate with their value?

Remember that not all data is made equal, and therefore not all data has the same value to the organization. As a result, your information categorization will play a key role in the development of your tailored information security requirements and subsequent security controls. Refer to Chapter 4, *Information Security Risk Management*, for a detailed explanation of information categorization.

Developing a security architecture advisement program

A well-defined security architecture advisement program will help to ensure that your information security program can provide reliable, high-quality, and repeatable guidance for your business and project stakeholders as it relates to supporting the development of information systems within your organization.

Partnering with your business stakeholders

To be successful, your architecture program must provide value to your business and project stakeholders and must not be an impediment to the project's success. A key component to ensuring success is to build in customer service as a guiding principle of your architecture program:

- Ensure that you have well-developed policies, procedures, and guidance to support your business and project stakeholders:
    - Develop policies that enforce the requirement for information security architecture and the need to request resources from the information security program for architectural guidance
    - Develop repeatable processes around how information security architecture is delivered to the organization
    - Develop templates and guidance so that you can easily gather the required information and develop the necessary outputs to make architectural decisions
    - Templated guidance that you should develop for your organization includes:
    - High-level and detailed information system design templates:
        - Contingency, business continuity, and disaster recovery templates
        - Configuration and change management templates
        - General and privileged user rules of behavior templates
        - System security plan templates
        - Security testing and planning templates
        - Risk assessment templates

- Ensure that you have a well-developed training program associated with information security architecture so that your business and project stakeholders understand:
    - What the information security program is providing in regards to the information security architecture services:
        - Ensure that you have repeatable training notes and slides that you can deliver to stakeholders
        - Explain the various services that are available (this will vary based on the maturity of your program)

    - How to best access these services and when they should access services:
        - Explain how the various stakeholders should interact with your architecture program in order to access services.

- Why they should care about the benefits of using information security architecture services and what these benefits are:
    - Be prepared to explain the benefits of information security architecture for the organization and how, by implementing a secure information system, we are all helping to ensure the success of our business missions.

Information security architecture process

A well-defined information security architecture process will follow the SDLC/SELC of your organization. If your organization does not have a well-defined SDLC/SELC process, then work to ensure that you are part of the project or task initiation within your various business operating groups.

What we are trying to ensure is that information security architecture is built into an information system at the earliest stage possible. The earlier that we can integrate with the stakeholders, the better we are able to serve their interests and the interests of the organization by developing the most secure system possible. Additionally, by starting earlier and building security into the system from the beginning, we are ensuring an integrated security solution rather than a bolted-on mess. This will help to ensure more efficient and better performing security controls.

Example information security architecture process

The following process provides an example of how to tie many of the concepts discussed in this chapter and in this book into an integrated information security architecture process that compliments an organization's SDLC/SELC process:

Task	Responsible party	Audience	SDLC phase
Request security architect	Project manager	Information security program	Initiation
Assignment of security architect	CISO/IT security manager	Information security program	Initiation
Contact project manager / team lead	Security architect	Project manager/ team lead	Initiation
Conduct meeting to kick off security architecture engagement	Security architect	Project manager / team lead / project team	Initiation
Conduct initial information security analysis	Security architect	Project manager / team lead / project team	Initiation
Provide tailored information security requirements	Security architect	Project manager / team lead / project team	Requirements analysis
Development and review of information system design. (Technical)	Security architect / project team	Project manager / team lead / project team	Design
Development and review of information operational and management-related information system artefacts	security architect / project team	Project manager / team lead / Project Team	Design
Develop Information Security Testing and Planning Documents	Security Architect	project manager / team lead / project team	Design

Support the implementation of the information system from an information security perspective	Security architect	Project manager / team lead / project team	Implementation
Conduct security testing	Security architect	Project manager / team lead / project team	Testing
Mitigate security testing findings	Project manager / team lead / project team	Security architect	Testing

Summary

In this chapter, we learned that information security architecture establishes rigorous and comprehensive policies, procedures, and guidelines around the development and operationalization of an information security architecture across the enterprise information technology deployed within an organization.

In this chapter, you learned:

- How to integrate information security architecture into the SDLC/SELC
- How to conduct an information security analysis that supports information security architecture decisions
- How to develop an information security architecture advisement program

In the next chapter, you will learn about information security considerations related to cloud computing implementations. You will learn about the various technologies that are present in the cloud and the tools and techniques needed to secure them.

Cloud Security Consideration

11

Cloud computing enables on-demand and ubiquitous access to a shared pool of configurable, outsourced computing resources, such as:

- Networks
- Servers
- Storage
- Applications

These services can be rapidly provisioned and released with little effort from the organization or cloud service provider.

Cloud computing characteristics

- **Rapid elasticity**: Cloud computing resources can be elastically provisioned and released. They can be scaled in the following ways:
    - **Manual scaling**: This is where the organization's operations team anticipates future workloads in the cloud environment and adds resources manually to support the organization's mission.

- **Semi-automated scaling**: This type of scaling still requires forecasting to ensure that resources exist and are built to support an organization's information system. Based on system events, new services, such as virtual servers to take the application's load, will be initialized.
- **Fully-automated (elastic) scaling**: This type of scaling allows an organization to increase or reduce capacity without the need to perform the manual labor and configuration necessary to establish the infrastructure ahead of time.

The organization has the capability of controlling the elasticity of the system so that the system does not grow out of control, causing a great fiscal impact.

- **Broad network access**: Access to the cloud resources is provided over the various network and user access devices, such as:
  - Workstations
  - Laptops
  - Mobile phones
  - Thin clients

A properly architected cloud environment provides increased network access and scalability.

- **On-demand self-service**: This refers to an organization's ability to provision cloud computing capabilities to include:
  - Storage
  - Processors
  - Memory
  - Guests

This callability can be executed without requiring human interaction from the cloud services provider.

- **Resource pooling**: The cloud provider utilizes a multitenant architecture where computing resources are pooled to serve multiple organizations. Pooled resources include:
    - Storage
    - Processing
    - Memory
    - Network bandwidth

Physical and virtual resources are dynamically assigned and reassigned based on the organization's requirements. The organization typically has no control over the exact physical location where services are provided. Based on the cloud service provider and the organization's requirements, the organization may be able to specify geographic locations at elevated levels in the contract, such as:

- State
- Country
- Data center

- **Measured service**: Pooled cloud computing resources are monitored and reported to the organization, providing:
    - Visibility into the consumption of cloud computing resources and their associated costs
    - Accurate measurement of cloud computing resource consumption
    - Transparency for both the provider and consumer of the cloud computing service

Cloud computing service models

There are three main cloud computing service models that we will be covering in this chapter. These three models provide the basis for the services provided by cloud computing service providers.

Infrastructure as a Service – IaaS

Infrastructure as a Service (**IaaS**) is a cloud computing service model where a provider delivers virtualized IT infrastructure resources over the internet:

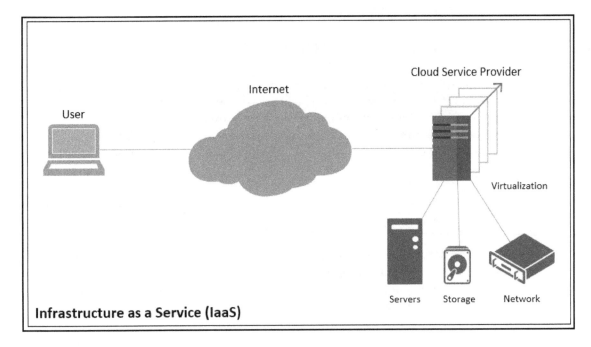

Infrastructure as a Service (IaaS)

The organization manages:

- Server operating systems
- Data storage
- Applications deployed to servers, such as:
    - Web-based enterprise applications
    - Database servers
    - Management agents, such as host intrusion prevention

The cloud computing service manages the underlying cloud infrastructure, which includes:

- Processing
- Physical storage
- Networks

Platform as a Service – PaaS

Platform as a Service (PaaS) is a cloud computing service model where a provider delivers hardware and software typically with the goal of supporting an organization's application development and hosting needs over the internet:

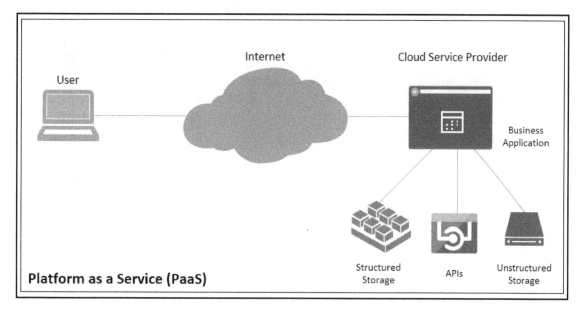

The organization manages:

- Applications deployed on the cloud computing infrastructure using:
    - Programming languages
    - Development libraries
    - Application services
    - Development tools

The cloud computing service also manages the underlying cloud infrastructure, which includes:

- Processing
- Physical storage
- Networks
- Operating system

Software as a Service – SaaS

Software as a Service (SaaS) is a cloud computing service model where a provider hosts a web-based application for the organization making it available to the organization over the internet:

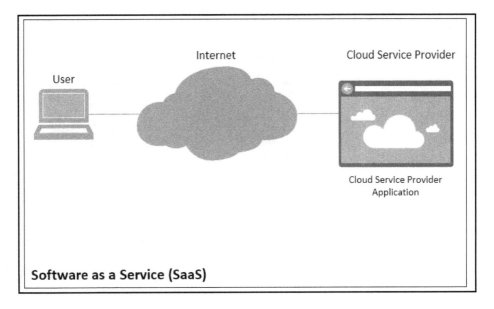

The organization manages:

- The data provided to the application environment
- Application configuration exposed by the application provider

The cloud computing service manages the underlying cloud infrastructure, which includes:

- Processing
- Physical storage
- Networks
- Operating system
- Enterprise applications

Cloud computing deployment models

The cloud computing deployment model will vary depending on your organization's unique business and mission requirements. The various deployment models bring their unique advantages, disadvantages, and information security challenges.

Public cloud

In this model, the cloud computing infrastructure is utilized by the public in a multitenant environment over the internet:

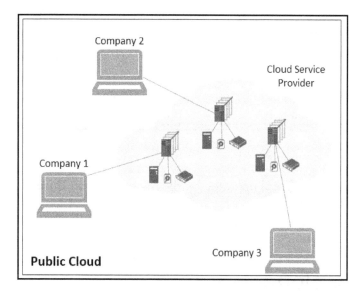

The service provider makes resources available, such as:

- Virtual machines (VMs)
- Applications
- Storage
- And so on

The cloud computing provider may be owned, managed, and operated by a business, academic, or government organization, or a combination of the three.

Private cloud

In this model, the cloud computing infrastructure is provisioned for exclusive use by a single organization, as illustrated in the following image:

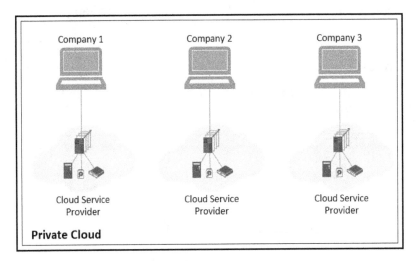

The cloud computing provider may be:

- Owned, managed, and operated by the organization, a third party, or a combination of the two
- It may exist on or off premises

Community cloud

In this model, the cloud computing infrastructure is provisioned for exclusive use by a specific community of consumers from organizations that have shared concerns (for example, mission, security requirements, policy, and compliance considerations), as shown in the following image:

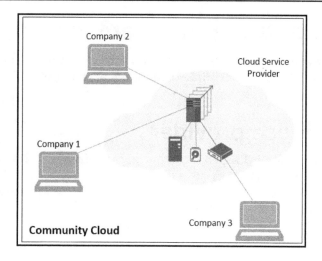

The cloud computing provider may be:

- Owned, managed, and operated by one or more of the organizations in the community, a third party, or a combination of the two
- It may exist on or off premises

Hybrid cloud

In this model, the cloud computing infrastructure is a combination of two or more cloud computing infrastructure types that remain separate from each other, but share the ability to exchange data and/or application information, as shown in the following image:

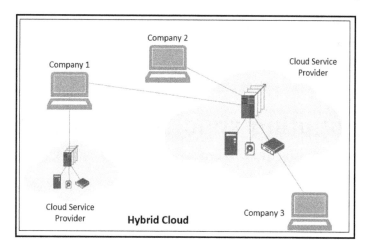

Cloud computing management models

The mechanism that you use to manage your cloud infrastructure must be well thought out and planned in order for your cloud implementation to be successful.

Managed service provider

A **managed service provider** (**MSP**) ensures that an organization's IT assets are operated and maintained. Some examples of these assets are:

- IT infrastructure (servers, network gear)
- Enterprise applications (e-commerce, databases)
- End user computing (workstations, management infrastructure)
- Security operations (SIEM, vulnerability scanning)

In the case of a cloud service, an MSP will ensure that services like these are maintained if they exist in a cloud environment, as well as provide services to manage the cloud infrastructure itself. If an organization lacks the experience or personnel to manage a cloud service, an MSP can be contracted to manage the cloud environment for the organization.

Cloud service provider

A **cloud service provider** (**CSP**) is the actual service provider of the cloud technology that you are using. These are the companies that offer the actual services that make up your organization's cloud computing architecture, which includes:

- **Infrastructure as a Service (IaaS)**
- **Platform as a Service (PaaS)**
- **Software as a Service (SaaS)**

Cloud computing special consideration

While the prevalent marketing hype that surrounds cloud technologies can make it sound easy to move to the cloud, the reality is that moving to the cloud can be very difficult from a business, technical and security perspective. It is easy to become complacent as you move to the cloud, but you must resist this temptation.

Cloud computing data security

The security of your organization's data is a key concern for your organization and the information security program. This does not change as you move your organization's data into the cloud. Moving your organization's IT infrastructure to the cloud will present you with many decisions around how to best secure your organization's information, such as those detailed in the following sections.

Data location

There are multiple concerns in data location that you need to consider when you approach your cloud computing services architecture. Some considerations include:

- Do your compliance requirements require your information to stay within a specific country or geographic region?
    - You will need to work with your cloud service provider to ensure that your data center is well defined and that your data stays within agreed data centers per your organization's requirements
- How are security controls applied across locations?
    - Do not take for granted that secure control of the application is ubiquitous across geographic locations. Work with the vendor to understand how data security controls are applied.
    - You need to know how your data moves between locations.
    - Ensure that you fully understand how data moves between cloud processing locations, ensuring that data security controls are preserved during data transmission.

Data access

Cloud computing provides a wide array of mechanisms for data to be accessed. Understanding the following questions from business requirements and technical implementation perspective will help to ensure a cloud computing environment that meets your user and information security requirements:

- How will your organization's data be utilized?
- Who will be accessing the data?
- What controls need to be in place to protect the data?

Some questions to consider related to data access include:

- How will your organization's information be utilized?
    - This goes back to understanding the needs of your business/mission and performing the necessary data categorization activities
    - Understanding your organization's data and its sensitivity to the organization's mission is critical to establishing an effective architecture that will meet your mission requirements
- Who will have access to the information?
    - Ensure that you address all potential data access requirements from a permissions and user roles perspective
- Where are users coming from?
    - Are users coming from your corporate network, partners, public Wi-Fi? Understand all your potential scenarios so that you can build strong conditional access policies.

Storage considerations

The data storage options available to you will vary based on the cloud computing service model you have chosen to go with (IaaS, PaaS, and SaaS). Additionally, you will find that there are varying levels of control you can have over your data and the underlying storage depending on the service model you have selected. As a result, you will have to select different methods to ensure that you are properly securing your organization's storage and will need to select the appropriate controls depending on the service model your organization selects for its cloud computing needs.

Storage types

There are many storage solutions that cloud services use to support their customers. Understanding the available storage solutions is important so that you can apply the appropriate security controls to the cloud service:

- **IaaS**: In this model, your service provider will be provisioning storage resources that support your overall cloud infrastructure. Storage resources will be allocated to virtualized hosts and, in most cases, presented to operating systems as file systems. IaaS storage types include:
    - **Object storage**: API or web-based file storage. Examples include Amazon S3 and Microsoft Azure.

- **Volume storage**: Acts physical hard drives and will attach to virtualization host software such as VMware or Linux kernel-based virtual machines.

- **PaaS**: In this model, the service provider provisions all aspects of the underlying infrastructure and exposes APIs that allow a developer to store data on the storage that has been provisioned by the cloud services provider. PaaS storage types include:
    - **Structured data storage**: Highly organized and searchable data.
    - **Unstructured data storage**: This data is not organized and does not lend itself well to a structured storage approach. Unstructured data includes text files, videos, and so on.

- **SaaS**: In this model, the cloud service provider configures the web-based application and the cloud storage as a single offering. The management of cloud storage will typically be through an administrative component of the web application.

Storage threats

Threats to cloud storage are like those experienced by organizational hosted systems. The difference is that addressing these threats may require additional creativity, since you do not have direct access to the underlying storage and therefore cannot ensure its protection. Threats to cloud computing storage include:

- **Regulatory noncompliance**: Either the CSP is misconfigured or is missing a component that ensures regulatory compliance
- **Unauthorized access**: Data is accessed because of misconfiguration, hacking, or an intentional act on the part of the CSP
- **Data exfiltration**: Data is removed due to misconfiguration, hacking, or an intentional act on the part of the CSP
- **Improper sanitization or destruction of data**: When a cloud asset is retired, data is not properly sanitized and could be exposed
- **Loss of data integrity**: Modification, destruction, or corruption of data

Storage threat mitigations

There are many technologies that can be used to mitigate the various threats associated with cloud-based storage solutions. We will look at a few such technologies in detail in the following sections.

Encryption

Encryption is a vital technology that ensures the confidentiality of data in the cloud is maintained. When implementing encryption capabilities for your cloud computing environment, you must ensure that the technologies deployed support:

- Your specific cloud platform
- Organizational policies and rules
- Business and mission objectives
- Regulatory requirements

Encryption use cases:

- **Data in transit**: Encryption should be used when data is moved inside and outside of the cloud
- **Data at rest**: Data that resides on cloud storage should be encrypted when stored to ensure that the data cannot be removed
- **Data destruction**: Once the useful life of cloud resources has been reached, encryption can be used to make data unrecoverable
- **Multitenancy**: Encryption can be used to ensure that separations between different customers in a multitenant cloud are better maintained
- **Compliance with regulatory requirements**: Many compliance standards require encryption at rest and in transit

Encryption challenges:

- **Encryption key management**:
  - In many cases, the encryption capability of a cloud infrastructure is fully managed by the CSP, including the encryption keys.
  - If the CSP manages your encryption keys, you will not be able to completely trust your encryption mechanisms as the CSP would retain the ability to unencrypt your organization's data.
  - You should manage your own encryption keys if your CSP allows you to perform this function. Additionally, you should establish customer key management as a requirement when selecting a cloud service provider.

- It is important to note that managing your own encryption keys does add an administrative burden to the IT organization and will need to be accounted for from a resources perspective.

- **Data in use**: Generally, when data is in use it is unencrypted somewhere in the information systems. The unencrypted data may reside in memory or physical/virtual storage. While this data is being processed, it is vulnerable to unauthorized disclosure to individuals with elevated privileges within the cloud computing infrastructure.

- **Performance**:

  - Encryption may negatively affect performance depending on the cloud computing implementation

  - Special attention will need to be given to high-performance and mission-critical applications to ensure that encryption technologies do not cause a denial of service due to the performance impact associated with encryption

- **Complexity**:

  - Encryption may have an impact regarding how data replication, backups, and disaster recovery occurs

  - Encryption must be developed that properly secures the information while ensuring that business/mission processes continue to function

Data loss prevention

The **data loss prevention (DLP)** tools are used to ensure that organizational data is properly maintained and controlled. Access to information being managed by a DLP system has the following features and arrangements:

- Tightly controlled with access controls
- Extensive logs are maintained to ensure visibility
- Rule sets are developed to generate alerts
- Data is prevented from being accessed in an unauthorized manner

The data loss prevention life cycle supports both the organization's requirement to protect intellectual property and the technical implementation of a data loss prevention tool as part of the enterprise network. The following are the stages of the life cycle:

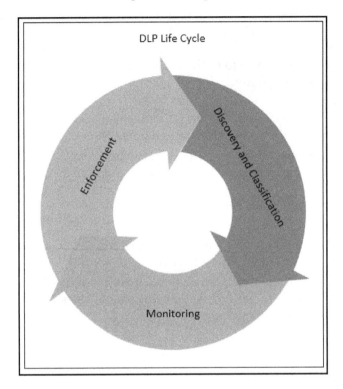

1. **Discovery and Classification**:
   - This is the first and most important stage of the DLP process
   - Without properly understanding your information, you have no means to understand which rules should be applied to your information
   - Utilize the guidance in this book related to data categorization
   - You will be mapping your internal information (intellectual property) to cloud computing architecture components (hardware/software)

2. **Monitoring**:
   - Your DLP system will monitor data usage from both an inbound and outbound perspective
   - Usage policies will be defined based on business requirements and data criticality
   - The DLP system must be architected to monitor all available ingress and egress options for your data

3. **Enforcement**:
  - This is where the DLP policies you previously established are enforced. Here, your DLP system will either allow or restrict access, and alert you to data requests
  - When a violation of a predefined policy occurs, the DLP system will then engage an enforcement action to protect organizational information
  - Enforcement actions include:
    - **Alerting**: Alerts can be sent to the administrator of the DLP system, managers, or the security operations center
    - **Logging**: Logging can be maintained for forensics purposes and forwarded to the SIEM for analysis by the security operation center
    - **Blocking**: Requests for information can be blocked
    - **Request additional permissions**: Workflow can be triggered to either positively identify the requesting user or required permission from someone else to access the information

Cloud computing DLP considerations

As you develop your architecture around DLP in your cloud computing environment, you will need to consider the following as regards policy:

- When is data allowed to leave the cloud environment?
- How should organizational data be stored and what precautions should the DLP system put in place related to storage?
- What kind of data should be stored in the cloud?
- Does your organization have information that should never be in the cloud environment?
- How should data be accessed?
  - Which networks?
  - Which devices?
  - Which applications?
- What compliance requirements, rules, and laws need to be enforced?

Managing identification, authentication, and authorization in the cloud computing environment

With the proliferation of cloud services and internal organizational IT resources, the need to manage your organizational user's identity is critical. Federating your organization's identity provider with your cloud services helps to ensure that your cloud services rely on a single source for identity whereby you can establish policies and ensure strong access controls, as shown in the following image:

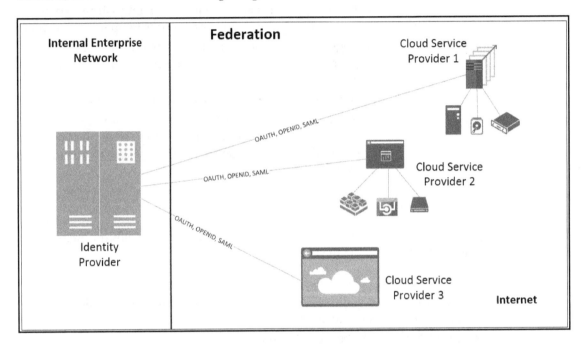

Identification considerations

Most modern cloud infrastructures have moved to standards-based identity providers so that identity can be easily shared between internal and external IT environments. The standards deployed by the various vendors include:

- **OpenID**: http://openid.net.
- **OAuth**: https://oauth.net/.
- **SAML**: Typically used in the enterprise environment to federate Microsoft Active Directory with cloud services. See https://en.wikipedia.org/wiki/Security_Assertion_Markup_Language for more information.

From a selection criteria perspective, if you are working with a cloud vendor and they do not support these standards, you should move to another vendor.

Authentication considerations

Authentication will take place as part of the federation between the cloud service and your backend enterprise directory service. You should consider adding multifactor authentication capabilities to your architecture when you move to federating your internal directory with external cloud services.

Once you federate with an external service, you have increased your overall threat surface as most cloud services will need to be accessible to the entire internet. This means that your username and passwords will be testable by malicious actors across each of your cloud platforms.

By adding a second factor to your authentication, you are ensuring that you need more information than just simply the username and password pair. The user associated with the account will need to be available and present to validate that they are attempting to log in. Studies have shown that implementing multifactor authentication greatly reduces the risk associated with username/password harvesting, which is of greater concern once a large portion of your IT infrastructure is exposed to the public internet.

Authorization considerations

Authorization typically takes place within the cloud service provider's infrastructure after identification and authentication have occurred. It is very important to remember that your cloud infrastructure must be actively managed and cannot be forgotten because it is being operated and maintained by the cloud service provider. Managing authorization within the cloud infrastructure is usually a customer responsibility and will not be accomplished by the cloud service provider.

Integrating cloud services with the security operations center

Ensuring that you have visibility into your cloud computing infrastructure from an information security perspective should be a top priority of the information security program when it comes to building an effective security cloud architecture.

As you begin to outsource your organization's information technology to cloud vendors, you must ensure that you do not comprise on information security control implementation. While you most likely will not be able to use the same solutions to implement information security as you did for on-premises solutions, you will be able to find satisfactory substitutes for use in the cloud environment.

Cloud access security brokers

The **cloud access security brokers** (**CASB**) is a very important technology to consider as you architect your cloud infrastructure. In fact, it will be very difficult to get an on-premises level of security, visibility, and security operations center integration into your cloud implementation without a tool like a CASB.

Many cloud service providers do not build the tools that you would wish for as an information security professional to manage the information security of the cloud environment. However, what many of the cloud service providers do is expose APIs that a third party can use to wrap the cloud solution in a layer of information security protections. These third-party vendors can use the cloud service provider APIs to:

- Control access to cloud resources
- Implement DLP functionality as part of the CASB
- Integrate with on-premises DLP systems
- Integrate behavioral analytics to detect unusual user behavior
- Many CASBs include on-premises components to detect shadow IT cloud usage
- Integrate with on-premises information security tools and the security operations center

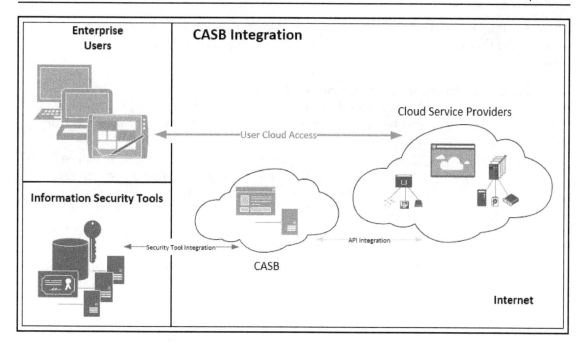

Cloud service provider API exposure should be another one of your purchasing criteria when you are looking for a new cloud solution to add to your cloud architecture. If the cloud service provider does not expose these APIs, move on to a vendor that does if it all possible.

Special business considerations

When you begin the planning phases of a cloud implementation, it is critical that you begin the discussion with your business/mission users and leaders ensure that they are part of the process from project initiation.

There are unique risks that present themselves as part of a cloud implementation, and you must ensure that your business organizations are willing to accept these risks. These risks include:

- **Unauthorized access to organizational data**:
    - Modern cloud service providers do an excellent job at operations and have developed an excellent arsenal of information security tools
    - However, there is a risk that a cloud service provider will be attacked either over the internet or through employee collusion because of the sheer volume of intellectual property they contain

- **CSP information security risks**:
    - There is an inherent trust that you place in the cloud provider when you entrust them with your organizational assets
    - Any information security risk that the cloud service provider has immediately becomes your information security risk as soon as you transition operations to the vendor

- **Organizational legal and compliance risks**:
    - Does your organization have any specific legal and compliance requirements that make it difficult or impossible for you to use the cloud service provider?
    - Does the CSP provide you with the access and control necessary to ensure that you are meeting your organizational obligations?

- **CSP management risks**:
    - Your organization has no control over whether the cloud service provider pays their bills or ensures that the equipment hosting your environment is well maintained and in good working order.
    - How does the cloud service provider communicate changes such as upgrades and feature updates?

- **Cloud service availability**
    - Your organization will no longer be able to plan for your information systems availability.
    - This will be fully managed by your cloud service provider. Is this acceptable to your business leaders?

Summary

In this chapter, you learned about cloud architecture and the considerations that go into planning out an effective and secure cloud implementation for your organization. Additionally, we discussed:

- Characteristics related to cloud computing
- Service, deployment, and management models utilized by cloud service providers
- Special considerations related to cloud data security

In the next chapter, we will be discussing information and data security best practices, and we will provide you with an understanding of many of the best practices needed to support effective IT hygiene in your organization's enterprise network

12
Information and Data Security Best Practices

In this chapter, we will round out the book by going over a selection of best practices to help ensure the overall information security health of your organization's information systems. Most of the best practices that I will be highlighting are foundational items related to your information system's overall health and should be addressed either before or in parallel to the implementation of advanced information security tools.

In this chapter, you will learn information security best practices related to:

- User account security
- Least functionality
- Updates and patching
- Secure configurations
- Application security
- Network security

Information security best practices

In this section, we will address information security best practices as they relate to both the server and workstations.

User accounts

User account management is critically important in a well-managed and secure enterprise information environment. It is important that you develop strong information security policies related to user accounts and their management, and develop mechanisms to audit your information system to ensure that your organization's policies are being followed.

Limit administrator accounts

Not everyone in your organization has administrator privileges on your information systems. The creation and assignment of administrative rights to your organization's team members should be carefully considered and given to only the people that need to have the permissions. When creating these accounts, bear in mind the following guidelines:

- Accounts with global impact, such as enterprise admins and domain admins, should be given to very few individuals:
    - Well-intentioned administrators can make serious, inadvertent misconfigurations on your enterprise network
    - Malicious administrators will essentially have full control over your network and can make changes and access information as they see fit
    - Provide the necessary permissions for administrators to do their daily jobs while ensuring access to elevated permissions is available if needed to address emergencies
- Create a strong password and disable the built-in local administrator's account in Windows:
    - This account is frequently targeted by malicious users because it can be attacked if it is renamed.
    - There are special cases where the built-in administrator account must be used for operating system changes. For this reason, make sure that you securely store the password so that it can be accessed in the future. Other than these special use cases, the built-in administrator account should not be used.
    - While you are at it, disable the built-in guest account following the same guidance given for the built-in administrator account.

Using a normal user account where possible

In most cases, an administrator account is not needed for most work done on the enterprise information system. Only a small percentage of your organization's workforce is performing IT administration as their primary job function, and as a result, they do not need to use an administrator account as their *daily driver* account:

- It is highly recommended that even IT administrators use a nonprivileged user account as their normal login:
    - The IT administrator would then elevate their privileges using the **Run as administrator** in Windows (as shown in the following screenshot) or sudo in Linux:

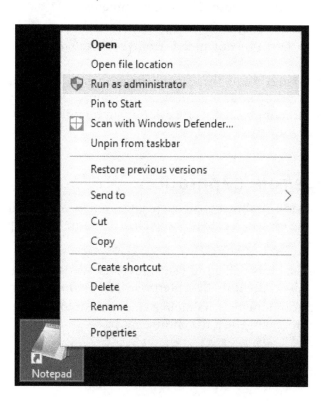

- Administrator accounts should be highly restricted for your general user populations or should be simply banned in your organization.
- Administrator accounts should not be used for daily office automation activities, such as:
    - Document creation
    - Email
    - Web browsing

These daily activities can be an entry point for malware into your environment through:

- Macro viruses in office documents
- Phishing and spear phishing attacks
- Drive-by downloads from websites

With an elevated account, these malware vectors can be greatly amplified and present a true risk to your organization. By simply requiring your users to use a normal user account for daily office automation work, you can greatly reduce your risk exposure to this type of threat.

Least privilege/role separation

Every individual that has a qualified business justification in your organization to have an administrator account in most cases does not require the same level of privileges as an administrator:

- Some administrators will administer enterprise-wide capabilities and need greater permissions within the enterprise information system
- Other administrators may maintain a single IT component and do not require permissions that will affect the entire enterprise

Ensure that you properly architect your administrator user roles as part of your information system design so that you properly separate administrative roles as part of operations and maintenance.

Password security

Establishment and enforcement of a strong password policy is critical to protecting your organization's information systems. You should address organizational policy and information system configuration related to:

- **Password history**: The number of unique new passwords that can be used by a user account before a previous password can be reused
- **Maximum password age**: The period over which a password can be used before it must be changed
- **Minimum password age**: The period over which a password must be used before the user can change it, preventing the user from immediately returning to an old password
- **Minimum password length**: The minimum length that the password must be for the information system to accept it
- **Complexity requirements**: Determines what type of special characters must be included in a password for it to be accepted as valid by the information system

The implementation of a strong password policy will have a direct impact on your user population and must be communicated well in advance for your user community to understand why it must be implemented and what they must do to meet the requirements.

Least functionality

Modern information systems provide a great deal of capability and flexibility to the organization. As you are designing your information system, it is important to understand not just what your information system needs to do to meet business requirements, but also the operating system functionality that is not required to meet those same requirements.

You will want to ensure that you are restricting the functionality of the information system so that it operates as required while not exposing any unneeded services that can be used by an attacker to exploit the system. To achieve this, do the following:

- Ensure that you have installed everything that you need for your information system to function as intended. This includes:
  - Operating systems complements
  - Support applications
  - Operations and information security management agents
  - APIs

- Uninstall or restrict any components that are not needed for the information system to operate as expected. This includes:
    - Default installed operating system components
    - Software or services that may be included as value-added components of the required application software
    - Testing tools that may have been installed during implementation to validate system capabilities

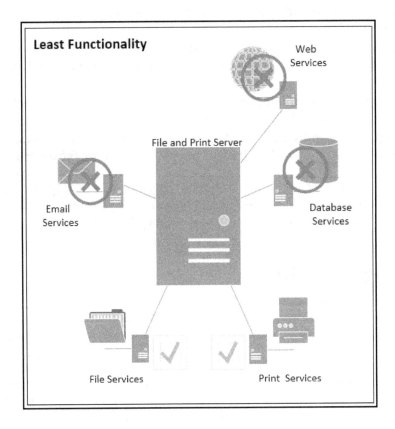

Updates and patches

One of the most important activities you can perform to ensure the security of your organization's information system is to keep your enterprise regularly updated with information security updates and patches provided by the various software vendors that make up your architecture.

To ensure that you have a well-developed patching program, you need to ensure that you have all the necessary components in place to ensure that you don't miss anything and that you are keeping all your software up to date. Your patching program should include the following:

- **Inventory**: An up-to-date inventory of your production information system that includes:
    - Server-specific information:
        - Operating systems:
            - Type
            - Version
        - Physical location
        - IP address

    - The person responsible for the maintenance of the information systems:
    - Installed server services:
        - Messaging services
        - Database services
        - Web services and so on

    - Installed applications:
        - Office automation software
        - Management agents

    The best way to conduct this type of assessment is through automation, as there are simply too many components to keep track of if you rely on manual verification and spreadsheets. You should utilize automated asset/configuration management tools to gather the aforementioned information.

- **Open source asset management tool examples**:
    - Snipe-IT: https://snipeitapp.com/download
    - OCS Inventory: https://www.ocsinventory-ng.org
    - GLPI: http://glpi-project.org
    - Fusion Inventory: http://fusioninventory.org

- **Standardize**: Standardize the applications and operating systems as much as possible across the information system. You have a better chance of success at properly patching your environment if you have fewer types of things to patch.

- **Prioritize**: Develop a thorough understanding of your network zones to understand how a specific vulnerability will impact your environment. When new patches for vulnerabilities are released by their vendors, you will need to provide guidance for your business regarding which patches must be installed first and what risks specific vulnerabilities pose to the organization. For example:
  - If two difficult-to-patch vulnerabilities are released at the same time, you must provide guidance regarding which patch will take top priority
  - One of the patches may be vulnerable to being exploited remotely, and you might discover that you have internet exposed systems that are vulnerable and need to be patched
  - The other patch might be exploited remotely, but the only affected systems are in a protected enclave within your internal network
  - In this case, you will prioritize the internet-facing servers for patching over the servers located within the protected enclave

- **Assess and classify**: Conduct assessments on your network on a periodic basis to develop a list of production systems that require patches. As with establishing an inventory, discovering which systems require patches should be achieved using automated tools. While it may seem appropriate to use patch management tools for this purpose, I recommend using a vulnerability management system:
  - Load a well-managed and maintained inventory from your asset/configuration management tools into your vulnerability management tool.
  - Assess your enterprise network for the existence of missing security patches.
  - Use the prioritization guidance that we looked at previously to classify the vulnerabilities identified due to missing patches, ensuring that critical patches with a likelihood of attack are on the top of that list. As you conduct this classification, consider the following:
    - What is the likelihood that the given threat will impact the organization's information system?
    - What is the likelihood that the given vulnerability can be exploited by a malicious actor?
    - What resources will be required to implement the patch?

- **Patch**: This may seem like a long way to go to patch your systems, but the reality is that the only way that you can guarantee that you will patch each system is through rigorous and reputable processes complemented by automation. Up to this point, you have:
    - Developed an accurate inventory so that you know what systems and applications assets you have
    - Standardized your information technology inventory as much as possible
    - Developed a mechanism to prioritize patch deployment
    - Assessed your technology assets for missing patches
    - Categorized missing patches to develop a patching deployment schedule
    - Now you are ready to deploy your patches utilizing you prioritized schedule

The best way to deploy patches, as with inventory and assessment, is through automation. You should utilize a patch management tool that supports all the various technologies that are utilized on your production network.

It is important to note that you may need more than one patch management system to patch your entire enterprise as not all technologies are supported by all patch management systems.

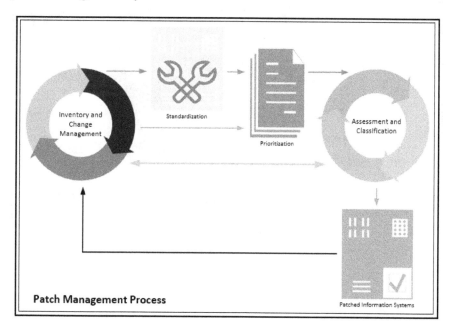

Patch Management Process

The importance of patching cannot be understated. The Equifax breach of 2017 is one of the largest privacy data breaches to occur and was preventable through adequate server patching (The *EQUIFAX OFFICIALLY HAS NO EXCUSE* article, dated September 9, 2014—https://www.wired.com/story/equifax-breach-no-excuse/).

Secure configurations

Securely configuring your information systems is a foundation IT hygiene management component that cannot be ignored. Unfortunately, far too often IT organizations overlook secure configuration, leading to an inevitable exposure of the organizational intellectual property.

The Verizon 2015 data breach report highlighted that 60% of all breaches could be traced back to information system misconfiguration, which clearly shows that this is a real and very serious problem:

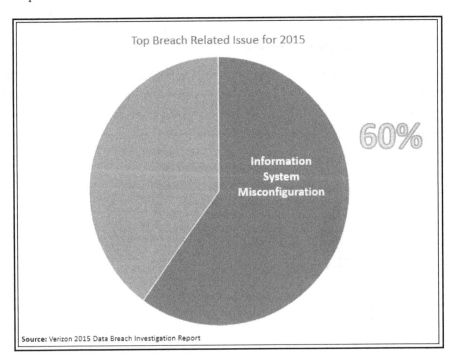

Developing a completely secure configuration strategy means that you should address the following components within your organization:

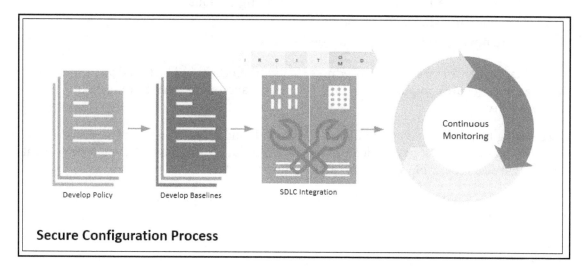

Secure Configuration Process

Step 1: Developing a policy that enforces secure configuration baselines

Ensure that your organizational policy enforces the need for secure configuration baselines and requires that information systems be configured in the most secure configuration that supports your business's needs and technical parameters.

Establish mechanisms that ensure that the information security program has a reporting capability to upper management that allows technical risks to be brought to the attention of senior leadership.

Step 2: Developing secure configuration baselines

Develop secure configuration baselines based on industry best practices, such as:

- **Center for Internet Security (CIS)**: https://www.cisecurity.org/
- **Defense Information Security Agency (DISA)**: https://iase.disa.mil

These organizations have developed detailed guidance, benchmarks, and procedures that explain the available security configuration options for a large range of applications, services, and operating systems.

The guidance contained within these documents includes:

- Enabling best practice security-related configurations
- Removal of unneeded accounts
- Removal or disabling of unneeded services

The guidance, benchmarks, and procedures that you select should be tested to meet your organization's security requirements, business needs, and operational technical supportability.

Once testing has concluded and you have developed tailored guidance that meets your organization's objectives, your tailed organization's guidance should be templated so that it can be used as a repeatable process for all new future systems.

This guidance should be followed for each technology type deployed as part of your enterprise information system.

If best practices guidance does not exist for a specific technology deployed by your organization, your information security program should work with business and IT stakeholders to develop guidance.

Step 3: Integrating secure configuration baselines into the SDLC

The information security program should work with business and IT stakeholders to ensure that secure configuration guidance is established throughout the SDLC life cycle for all information system environments, including:

- **Development**: Development environments tend to have more freedom so that experimentation and creativity can be fostered. As a result, many security vulnerabilities exist.

  Ensure that you protect your other information systems from your development environments and that you do not allow your development system to be inadvertently accessed from external parties.

  Development systems often contain extensive intellectual property and need to be well protected.

- **Testing**: Testing environments may be as well secured as production, or they may be as open as development. It really depends on your organization. Either way, protection decisions must be made at the level of enterprise.
  There are plenty of examples where old test servers were left internet exposed causing an avenue of entry into the organization.

  The Hackers breach security of *HealthCare.gov* article, dated September 04, 2014—https://www.nytimes.com/2014/09/05/us/hackers-breach-security-of-healthcaregov.html.

- **Production**: Ensure that your production environment is fully integrated with the guidance, benchmarks, and procedures developed to ensure secure configuration in your enterprise information systems. Deviations should never be based on convenience.
  If deviations need to occur because of business needs, mitigating/compensating controls should be applied to ensure the security of the enterprise information systems.

- **SDLC integration**: Integrating secure configuration as part of the SDLC will help to ensure that information systems are designed and configured in a secure fashion:

  - **Initiation: conduct analysis of business needs**:
    Working with your business and technology stakeholders you will develop a good understanding of what their needs are and what technologies will be used for their information system.

  - **Requirements analysis: baseline review and development**:
    At this point in time, you will be able to determine if you have the necessary baselines to support the required technology.
    Any baselines that do not exist should be developed to support the new information system's design process.

  - **Design: incorporate baselines into the design**:
    Ensure that the design fully incorporates the prescribed baselines. Deviations should never be based on convenience.
    If deviations need to occur because of business needs, mitigating/compensating controls should be applied to ensure the security of the enterprise's information systems.

  - **Implementation: testing updates and emergency changes**:
    Not all baseline settings will work in the production environment because of unforeseen complexities and interactions.
    Support your implementation team with mitigating/compensating controls if it is found that planned baseline controls will not work in the production environment.

- **Testing: conduct automated assessment**:
  Validate that the baseline controls have been fully implemented
  and that they are functioning as expected using an automated
  assessment tool, such as a vulnerability scanner.
- **Operations: continued automated assessments**:
  Periodically conduct an automated assessment of the information
  system's baseline security settings, ensuring that the settings stay
  configured as expected.
  Test any new updates and changes to the information systems,
  ensuring that baseline configuration settings are applied to these
  changes.
- **Disposition: sanitize and test media**:
  Conduct media sanitization to ensure that organizational
  intellectual property and sensitive files are fully removed from the
  information system.
  Test the information system's media to validate that information is
  not forensically retrievable.

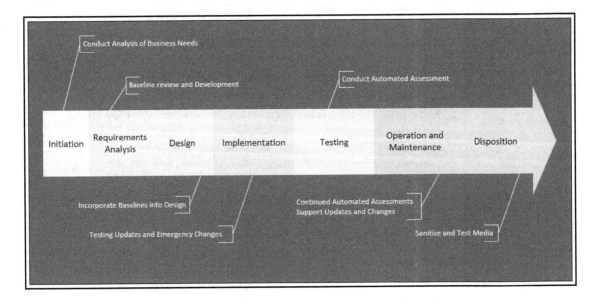

Step 4: Enforcing secure configuration baselines through automated testing and remediation

To ensure secure configurations throughout the useful operational life of your information systems, you must ensure that you are adequately conducting continuous monitoring of your information security controls.

Information systems lose their secure configurations for many reasons:

- Updates to software may unexpectedly remove a secure configuration
- During an update, a secure configuration may inadvertently not be applied
- Secure configurations may not be applied during an update for convenience
- A secure configuration may be removed for testing purposes and not reapplied, or a mitigating/compensating control may not be applied if it is found that the secure configuration may be causing a mission impact.

In these cases, the offending configuration must be identified and repaired to ensure the continued security of the organization.

Application security

Web applications need special care and attention. This is a technology with which it is very easy to establish vulnerabilities that can be exploited easily.

Conducting a web application inventory

Understanding what web applications your organization has in its inventory is very important. Early in this chapter, we discussed the importance of developing a complete inventory so that we could better protect our environment. It will be very difficult to maintain an effective application security program without having detailed knowledge of the applications implemented throughout your organization. You should strive to answer questions such as:

- How many total applications are in the organization?
- What programming languages do they use?
- What tier architecture do they use?

- Where are they located within the enterprise infrastructure?
- Who manages the applications?
- What is the purpose of the applications?

Make sure that you gather as much information about the applications as you can so that you have the details needed to go back to the responsible parties when it the time comes to discuss information security issues.

Least privileges

When developing web applications, ensure that you only provide the applications on the information system with the most minimal set of privileges necessary for the application to operate.

Each application that is developed for your environment has permissions that are very specific to the information system they are installed on. If a vulnerability exists within the information system and that vulnerability can be exercised by an attacker, then the attacker would be controlling an exploited system with the permissions of the web application. If the application was running with administrative permissions, then the attacker would be running with those permissions. Therefore, it is imperative that you ensure that your web applications run with the smallest set of permissions possible to enhance the overall security of the application.

Cookie security

Cookies are often an overlooked item when it comes to application security. However, improper use of cookies can disclose sensitive application information and provide access to privileged application locations.

When using cookies, remember a few basics:

- Do not use cookies to store sensitive user or application information
- Encrypt sensitive information contained within cookies

Web application firewalls

A web application firewall is a security tool that sits between a user request and a web application. The web application firewall can intercept and inspect packets intended for a web application and analyze those packets for attack patterns.

The web application firewall:

- Monitors user requests
- Filters those requests based on administratively defined rules
- Blocks web-based requests to web applications that could potentially cause harm

Web application firewalls are typically used to block web-based application from threats that include:

- SQL injection
- Cross-site scripting
- Session hijacking
- Resource access

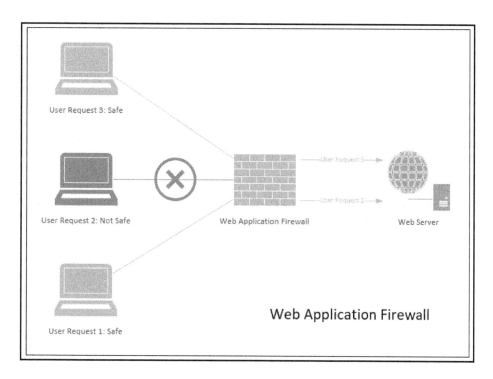

There are two types of web application firewall that can be used from an architectural perspective:

- **Cloud WAF**: A cloud WAF exists as software as a service and is not managed on premises. These types of service require that you redirect the web traffic destined for your web application to the cloud WAF provider. The cloud WAF service then analyses all web traffic for malicious content prior to delivering the requests to your web application.
- **On-premises WAF**: This is an appliance, virtual machine, or software that you manage on-premises and integrates into your application architecture. This type of WAF operates in a similar way to the cloud WAF, except that you are responsible for the operations and management of the complete WAF solution (hardware and software) rather than just being responsible for the WAF application configuration.

Implementing a secure coding awareness program

Engage your organization's software development community with the necessary training and tools so that they can build secure applications. In most cases, your team members are very conscientious and want to do a great job for your organization. If your application development group is consistently developing insecure software, they may lack the necessary skills to identify the insecure code.

By establishing a training program, you will give your developers the ability to identify and remediate vulnerabilities in their software as it is being developed. This will greatly decrease the development time for the software as new application code will not need to be stuck in multiple cycles of security testing and remediation to be approved for production.

This training will serve to provide the application developers with the tools to prevent the web application vulnerabilities that are so prevalent in modern web applications, such as:

- SQL injection
- Cross-site request forgery
- Cross-site scripting

Network security

Securely configuring your network hardware and configurations will ensure that you have an effective and secure communication infrastructure. Bear in mind the following principles and guidelines:

- **Ports, protocols, and services**:
    - Ensure that you extend the concepts of least privilege and least functionality to the network.
    - Block any outbound traffic that is not required as this can be used to exfiltrate data from your network.
    - The same goes for inbound traffic. If you do not need a port, protocol, or service to be open, close it.

- **Traffic monitoring**:
    - Ensure that you are monitoring the outbound ports that you allow with a full packet capture and analysis capability to ensure that the traffic that is leaving your network is legitimate.
    - For encrypted traffic, add an SSL decrypter to your network. Run this traffic through your security tool suite, including your full packet capture tools, to detect and alert you to potential malware activity.
    - These tools should all roll up into your security operations center for analysis by your SOC analysts.

- **SNMP**:
    - Change the default community strings to an organizationally defined string
    - Establish authorized SNMP management stations
    - If SNMP is not required, then turn off the service

- **VLAN**:
    - VLANs should be used to isolate and segment your network
    - Network segmentation examples include:
        - Internal servers
        - DMZ
        - Workstations
        - Security devices
        - Management network

- **Promiscuous mode**:
    - Establish restriction on network equipment so that promiscuous mode network devices cannot collect packet data from the enterprise network without authorization.

Remote access

Remote access into your network exposes a secure mechanism, allowing remote users to access internal resources. If this is not handled properly, you could be exposing your internal network to attackers. Adhere to the following principles and guidelines to avoid this:

- **Do not allow unapproved VPN access methods**:
    - Establish a policy stating that there is only a single mechanism for remote access and stating who administers that method
    - Establish a secured VPN capability and do not allow users to utilize an alternative mechanism
    - Assign users access to the VPN capability based on business need and not personal desire
- **Block split tunneling**:
    - All network traffic should be required to go through the VPN
    - This means that web requests would go through the VPN and out the corporate network rather than the local Wi-Fi access point.
- **Multifactor authentication**:
    - Utilize multifactor authentication to protect the user's authentication credentials
    - Second factors that can be utilized include:
        - Smart cards
        - Certificates
        - Physical tokens
        - SMS/text messages

Wireless

Implementing strong wireless controls will ensure that your sensitive organizational information will be secured while also ensuring that you can provide simplified access for your visiting guests and organizational partners. Bear in mind the following guidelines when establishing wireless controls:

- **Authentication**: Utilize 802.1x for authentication, ensuring that only approved devices are permitted to connect to the enterprise wireless network.
- **Guest Network**: Establish a guest network on your wireless infrastructure for:
  - Visiting customers
  - Business partners
  - Vendors

  Do not allow connectivity between the guest network and your organization's internal network. Authorized users of your guest network should only be allowed to connect to the internet. Ports, protocols, and services should be restricted, and network traffic should be monitored per your organizational policy to prevent malicious activity.

- **SSID**:
  - The SSID utilized by your wireless network should not be easily associated with your organization
  - Suppress the wireless network from broadcasting the wireless network SSID

- **Encryption**:
  - Use the strongest encryption available on your wireless infrastructure
  - WPA2 Enterprise is the currently recommended encryption method
  - Do not use WEP

Mobile devices

Mobile devices are a way of life in the modern enterprise. Establishing policy and security controls are an important step in ensuring the security of organizational data on mobile devices. Bear in mind the following guidelines and principles when dealing with mobile devices:

- **Develop a mobile device policy**: A mobile device policy is an important part of an organization's ability to manage its overall information security posture.
- **Inventory**: Identify mobile devices maintaining an inventory, ensuring that unauthorized devices do not obtain access to organizational resources.
- **Mobile device management**: Utilize a centralized management tool managed by the organization to ensure mobile device compliance with organizational policies.
- **Establish secure communications for mobile devices**: Ensure that every aspect of mobile device connectivity is accounted for and that all communications channels that will carry organizational data are encrypted.
- **Passwords**: You need to configure the requirement of a password to access the device.
- **Remote wipe**: Enable remote device wipe, which allows administrators to completely wipe the mobile device if the device is lost or stolen.
- **Encryption**: Enforce device encryption to protect organizational data at rest.
- **Containerization**: Segregate enterprise and personal information. This allows IT operations to control how organizational data is used on the mobile device without affecting employee personal information.
- **Antivirus**: Android and iOS are ever-increasing targets for malware. Antimalware software should be used on any mobile device that processes organizational data. This software provides:
  - Real-time antivirus protection
  - Automatic updates of definitions
  - Firewall protection

Summary

In this chapter, we discussed a selection of best practices to help ensure the overall IT hygiene of your organization's information systems. We discussed concepts such as user account security, least functionality, updates and patching, secure configurations, application security, and network security.

Index

S

CPSIA information can be obtained
at www.ICGtesting.com
Printed in the USA
LVHW061313281122
734159LV00027B/373